The Secret Squadrons

The Secret Squadrons

Special Duty Units of the RAF and USAAF
in the Second World War

Robert Jackson

Robson Books

FIRST PUBLISHED IN GREAT BRITAIN IN 1983
BY ROBSON BOOKS LTD., BOLSOVER HOUSE,
5-6 CLIPSTONE STREET, LONDON WIP 7EB.
COPYRIGHT © 1983 ROBERT JACKSON

Jackson, Robert
 The secret squadrons.
 1. Great Britain *Royal Air Force* Special duty squadrons
 2. World War, 1939-1945—Aerial operations, British
 I. Title
 940.54'491   D786

 ISBN 0-86051-207-X

Printed in Hungary

Contents

Preface

Any aviation historian who has worked his way through the pages of the Operations Record Books of RAF squadrons for the period 1939-45 cannot have failed to notice one peculiarity. At the beginning the ORBs are usually comprehensive, containing detailed accounts of operations — and often little snippets of a personal nature — which prove invaluable to the researcher whose main interest is accuracy; but as the war progresses, the ORBs grow progressively more terse and laconic in their recording of events. A kind of tiredness creeps into them, as though the Intelligence Officers who compiled them wished for nothing more than to be done with it all. It is as though the weariness of the aircrew whose names appear in the pages of an ORB is reflected throughout the whole structure of an operational squadron, from the highest to the lowest echelons, even leaving its imprint on the day-to-day record of their exploits.

In the case of the Special Duties Squadrons, there is added another ingredient to make the researcher's task more difficult: the obvious need for secrecy. This need was so urgent that, in some instances, operations went unrecorded, and in others there are unaccountable gaps in the ORBs; those for No. 138 Squadron, for example, covering the vital period from July to November 1944 — when the Squadron suffered some of its heaviest losses over Poland — are missing.

Of necessity, therefore, some squadrons have received more

coverage in this book than others, simply because more material is available on their activities. No. 161 Squadron's ORB, for example, is excellent, setting forth painstaking details of all the unit's operations, with particular reference to Lysander and Hudson pickup operations in France; on the other hand, No. 148 Squadron's Lysander missions to Greece appear only in sparse detail. This in itself is not particularly important, for pickup operations in Greece did not differ greatly from those in France, apart from local weather conditions; in Burma, however, it was a far different story, and in this case I have luckily been able to compile a fairly comprehensive account of what has hitherto been a much-neglected phase of RAF special duties work.

At this stage, I should point out that this is not a story of the Special Operations Executive, or any of the other clandestine organizations that worked alongside it. Excellent accounts of their activities, and of the gallant men and women who served with them, are to be found elsewhere, and I have supplied a bibliography for anyone wishing to undertake further reading. This is the story of the aircrews, the aircraft and the squadrons that operated in support of SOE and its kindred organizations, and in so doing wrote a unique and courageous chapter in the annals of air warfare. At a distance of forty years, the skill of those special duties crews, penetrating deep into the heart of occupied Europe in search of the tiny pinpricks of light that marked their dropping or landing zones, or seeking a minute clearing amid the forests of South-East Asia, often with no navigational aid other than a map and the keenness of their eyes, seems incredible; and yet they did it, time after time, and succeeded in their task.

The contribution made by the clandestine organizations to the eventual Allied victory was enormous; in France alone, it has been estimated that the effort they produced was worth that of at least six divisions — and that effort was supported, for most of the war, by only two Royal Air Force squadrons in that particular theatre. Multiplied by the efforts of Allied special duties squadrons in other theatres of war, there can be no doubt that clandestine air operations had a significance which, perhaps, has never been fully realized.

I have received assistance from many quarters in the preparation of this book. I should like, however, to extend my particular thanks to the Air Historical Branch (RAF) at the Ministry of Defence, and especially to Mr Humphrey Wynn of that Department, whose willingness to help is always unfailing.

Introduction

The infiltration of agents into enemy territory to gather intelligence and commit acts of sabotage is a process as old as the history of warfare. All that has really altered over the past century is the nature and sophistication of the equipment at an agent's disposal for transmitting vital data, and the means of getting him to his destination.

The use of aircraft in connexion with clandestine operations is by no means a product of the Second World War. In 1870, at the height of the Franco-Prussian War, balloons were used to fly both agents and secret documents out of besieged Paris, and there is some evidence to indicate that Italian airmen may have picked up agents from behind enemy lines during the brief war with Turkey in 1912.

The importance of aircraft in clandestine operations was quickly realized by both sides from the very beginning of the First World War, and secret flights across the lines were undertaken on a large scale throughout the conflict. From time to time, statements appeared in official Allied communiqués to the effect that the enemy were using aircraft to land spies and secret agents, and although there were never any official indications that the Allies were doing exactly the same, some reference to special missions occasionally crept into the press through an oversight of the censors. On 13 December 1914, for example, the *Observer* reported that a French pilot had landed a scout in German territory and brought him back again, and in the *Daily Telegraph* of 9 July 1915, a war correspondent named A. Beaumont reported from Italy that an Italian pilot had landed an observation officer behind the enemy's lines and had returned to pick him up a few days later.

In October 1915, HQ 7th German Army Corps issued an order directing that all landings of aircraft should be reported immediately, that any passengers should be detained or, if they had left the vicinity, that a search should be mounted for them. In the same month, the Germans claimed that Allied pilots had been landing soldiers in civilian clothing behind the lines to carry out sabotage against the German railway system.[1]

Official British references to the work of secret agents and the pilots who flew them into enemy territory were found only in occasional veiled references to intelligence duties in citations for honours and awards. On 14 November 1916, for example, the *London Gazette*, notifying the award of the DSO to 2nd Lieutenant C.A. Ridley, MC, of the Royal Flying Corps, stated that it was given 'for judgement in the execution of a special mission. When his machine was wrecked he showed great resource and obtained valuable information.' The true nature of Ridley's mission, however, does not appear in any official records.

Usually, clandestine air operations during the 1914-18 War were carried out on an ad hoc basis by whatever aircraft and pilots were available, many leading British and French pilots undertaking this kind of mission during their careers; for example, France's celebrated Georges Guynemer flew two secret missions, while another ace, Jean Navarre, carried out three. It is recorded that, of the three agents landed by Navarre, two were captured by the Germans and shot, while the third made his way back through neutral Holland.[2] On the other hand, some pilots specialized in clandestine work; one such was Jules Vedrines, the famous French pioneer airman of pre-1914 days, who received none of the limelight that was shed on men such as Guynemer and who — although he undertook many hazardous secret operations — was never mentioned in the official communiqués. This, in fact, led to the unfortunate Vedrines' courage being called into question by the uninformed, which prompted the French Government to drop a broad hint that the pilot was engaged in some sort of intelligence activity; a hint that produced the unexpected rumour that Vedrines was actually a German spy![3]

An excellent description of clandestine air operations during the 1914-18 War was given by a French author, M. Mortane, in a work that appeared in 1919. He wrote:

> This 'job of work' consisted of taking by aeroplane into enemy territory a passenger who would harvest information there, or, failing that, would employ dynamite to abolish important structures. The risk was great; a pilot captured at the moment of setting down his spy was liable to the death penalty — his companion was *sure* of being shot. One can imagine the courage required by these men setting out to alight in an unknown country as best they might, well knowing that the least failure of the machine would make return impossible ... The passengers were generally civilians, natives of the district which was being studied, customs officers or occasionally soldiers, who, with unusual knowledge of the country, or being avid of adventure, wished to tempt chance.
>
> There were two ways of setting about a special mission: to drop your spy and come back without bothering any more about him, or to go and look for him a few days later, the second method being rarely resorted to. The passengers took with them carrier-pigeons, by means of which they were able to transmit the information picked up from day to day. Then, when their task was finished, they would generally work back by way of Holland.[4]

Sometimes, the pilot assigned to landing an agent behind enemy lines would be notified whether it was safe to land or not by a system of signals displayed by an accomplice on the ground. One RFC officer described a case where signals were displayed by a harmless-looking old peasant woman in the form of washing spread out on a field. The woman turned out to be German, and the pilot narrowly escaped when concealed enemy troops opened fire on his aircraft.[5]

Sometimes, a considerable quantity of equipment was landed with the agent. Mortane tells how, in October 1918, a French aircraft landed two agents together with a supply of bully beef, biscuits and coffee, as well as a wireless mast, a transmitter, carrier-pigeons and dynamite. Another French officer, Lieutenant B.A. Molter, described how a member of his squadron, Adjutant Batcheler, took off one day on a clandestine operation carrying an agent who was dressed as a Walloon peasant; the man appeared to be a hunchback, but the 'hump' was in reality a cleverly-disguised wicker basket containing carrier-pigeons. The man was landed in a field fifteen miles behind the enemy lines; Batcheler quickly took off and headed for home, accompanied by two French aircraft which had been detailed to escort him.

Towards the end of the war, many agents were dropped by parachute rather than landed. In the summer of 1918, the Canadian pilot Major W.G. 'Bill' Barker, who was later to win the Victoria Cross for a gallant single-handed dogfight against fifty enemy aircraft over Flanders, set out from an Italian airfield to drop an agent named Tandura behind the Austrian lines; the plan was to land the man in some remote area from which he could make his way to Vittorio, collecting as much military information as possible en route and transmitting it by carrier-pigeon to the Italian forces.

Barker and Tandura were accompanied by a Captain Wedgwood Benn,* who was to act as navigator and despatcher. Tandura sat above a trapdoor built into the bottom of the fuselage; this could be released by a wire controlled by Captain Benn. Three bombs were also carried, two of them to be dropped after the agent had been released and the third to be retained in the machine as proof that Barker and Benn had been engaged on what Benn later described as 'a legitimate act of war' should they be forced down in enemy territory.

Tandura, a tough little mountaineer, wore Italian Army uniform but carried peasant's clothing in a knapsack. Following a safe landing, he operated behind the enemy lines from August to October 1918, gathering information of such value that the Italians regarded him as one of the principal architects of their success in the Battle of Vittorio and awarded him the Gold Medal for Valour, the Italian Army's highest decoration for gallantry. On one occasion, he was captured by Austrian

*Captain Wedgwood Benn later became 1st Viscount Stansgate. He was the father of the Rt Hon. Anthony Wedgwood Benn, MP.

soldiers, but passed himself off as an escaped prisoner of war and was put on labouring duties. He escaped after a couple of weeks and resumed his intelligence-gathering operations. It is probably no exaggeration to say that Tandura's efforts represent the finest example of the valuable work done by an agent infiltrated by air in the whole of the First World War.[6]

Generally, the identities of the agents they carried were unknown to this early generation of special duties pilots. The French pilot C.H.A. André recalled in his war memoirs one agent who was known simply as 'SSR 58'; he later discovered that this man was a French nobleman who assumed the identity of a peasant during his special missions. All the pilots who flew him over the lines knew was that they set him down and then returned at night to a pre-arranged field, where they waited for a signal — a light visible only from directly overhead — before landing to pick him up. On return to base, he would climb from the aircraft without a word and disappear into a waiting staff car; no one had the remotest idea what he did beyond the lines.[7]

Parachuting was a very new science in the 1914-18 War, and some agents were understandably afraid to launch themselves into space and place their trust in a thin silken canopy. The pilots of No. 60 Squadron, RAF, who — despite being fighter pilots in a unit equipped with SE.5s — were sometimes called upon to drop agents from elderly BE and FE aircraft in 1918, overcame this problem by making the agent sit on the trapdoor in the fuselage floor; when the pilot pulled a toggle, the trapdoor opened and the agent fell through. There was one story of a terrified agent, clinging to the sides of the cockpit for dear life, being beaten over the fingers with the butt of his pilot's pistol until he eventually let go.[8]

Landing or parachuting an agent into enemy territory was one thing; picking him up was quite another, and pilots involved in this type of operation sometimes had very narrow escapes. The French fighter ace René Fonck, of the famous Escadrille des Cigognes, told how a colleague was given the task of picking up an agent who carried vital information; the pilot landed at a pre-arranged rendezvous and waited for half an hour in brilliant moonlight before the agent finally appeared, hotly pursued by German troops. The pilot took off under heavy fire, which wounded the agent and riddled the aircraft. The pilot staggered back to the right side of the lines, where he made a forced landing.[9]

Another pilot damaged his propeller when landing to pick up an agent. The latter obligingly handed him a pigeon, which was dispatched with a scribbled note asking for someone to fly over with a spare propeller. Unfortunately the weather turned bad, and the expected aircraft failed to arrive. After waiting for three days, the pilot and agent were captured; the pilot, whose name was Clerisse, managed to escape, but the agent was presumably shot.[10]

On many occasions, pilots landed agents and then waited in the vicinity while the agent carried out some act of sabotage before taking him to safety again. On one occasion in 1915, a pilot of the RFC landed a BE.2c at night behind the enemy lines, some distance from a bridge that was to be blown. His passenger, an Engineer officer, waded along the river and placed a package of explosives against one of the bridge's key supports. While he was doing this, the pilot took off again and flew low over an enemy camp nearby, machine-gunning and dropping small bombs to create a diversion. Then he headed back to the landing field, picked up the soaking-wet sapper and climbed away towards friendly territory, accompanied by a highly satisfying 'crump' as the bridge went up in smoke.[11]

Several missions of this kind were carried out in Iraq. On 13 November 1915, Captain T.W. White of the Australian Flying Corps and Captain F.C.C. Yeats-Brown of the Indian Army flew a BE.2 sixty miles to a point in enemy territory close to Baghdad, their mission to destroy telegraph lines running to Constantinople. White unfortunately made a poor landing and smashed one wing of the aircraft, and although records state that Yeats-Brown succeeded in blowing up the wires the two officers came under fire from a party of Turkish troops and were taken prisoner.[12] At about the same time, a second BE.2 flown by Major Reilly, RFC, set out for a point beyond Baghdad, the mission of Reilly and his passenger being to blow up the railway line that was bringing Turkish troop reinforcements to the area. The aircraft, however, forced-landed in the desert a long way short of its objective, and the crew were captured by Arabs.[13]

Lieutenant-Colonel J.E. Tennant, DSO, MC, commanding No. 63 Squadron in Mesopotamia, described another

15

clandestine operation which was carried out at a later date:

> General Maude put forward the proposition that as . . . the
> enemy were evacuating their heavy stores and guns from
> Baghdad to Samarra by the railway, the interruption of
> that line might have far-reaching results. So on the 7th [of
> March 1917] two specially selected Engineer officers,
> Captains Cave-Brown and Farley, with charges of
> dynamite, left the ground piloted by Lieuts. Windsor and
> Morris. They managed to land within 200 yards of a
> railway culvert and kept their engines running. An Arab
> village lay about 800 yards away, and as soon as the RE
> officers got out of the machines Arab horsemen came
> galloping down on them. They bolted half-way to gain the
> culvert, but seeing that the game was obviously impossible,
> and also realising that their charges were insufficient to
> wreck the structure, they turned and ran back to the
> aeroplanes under fire from the Arabs. Both pilots, with
> their Lewis guns firing, took off straight into the enemy and
> got away. It was a near shave to losing the lot.[14]

The Germans were also actively engaged in this type of
operation. On the Eastern Front, according to one German
communiqué of the time, a Leutnant von Cossel was landed
behind enemy lines south-west of Rovno on 4 October 1916 in
an aircraft piloted by Feldwebel Windisch, and picked up again
twenty-four hours later. In the intervening period, von Cossel
blew up the railway line between Rovno and Brody at several
points.

In April and May 1917, German airmen serving with the
Turkish forces in Palestine made daring attempts to destroy
water conduits that were vital to the British forces in their
advance on Jerusalem. On 26 April, Hauptmann Felmy and
Oberleutnant Falke flew two aircraft to a point sixty miles
behind the British lines at Salmana in the Sinai Peninsula, and
while one of them pinned down a British patrol with machine-
gun fire the other blew up a water-pipe and a nearby railway
line. Both aircraft took off under fire and returned to their base.
A second raid, carried out by the same two men on 27 May, was
less successful. They landed at Bir-el-Abd in an attempt to cut

the railway and water pipeline, but were surprised by a patrol just as they were preparing to place their explosive charges and were forced to run for it, leaving behind their aircraft and equipment. The fate of the two airmen is not recorded.[15]

Although agents landed behind the enemy lines to gather intelligence usually wore civilian disguises, personnel infiltrated to carry out acts of sabotage normally wore military uniform in the hope that this would enable them to escape the firing squad (which it rarely did) if they were captured. There were, however, a few exceptions. On 20 October 1918, for example, Sous-Lieutenant Emrich of the French Flying Corps set out with two passengers — both soldiers but both wearing civilian clothes — for a field in Lorraine, the mission being to blow up a railway tunnel at Laifour. However, the aircraft was ambushed as it landed and put out of action, so Emrich set fire to it and made his escape, accompanied by the two saboteurs. Determined to complete their mission, they made for the rail tunnel only to find that it was virtually disused, most of the enemy traffic moving by way of a canal near the River Meuse, so instead they decided to use their explosives to destroy a lock gate. This they achieved successfully, eventually regaining French territory after spending nineteen days behind the enemy lines.[16]

Although pilots no doubt realized the importance of clandestine work, they mostly viewed it with distaste. In the 1914-18 War 'spy' was still very much a dirty word, particularly within the somewhat upper-crust atmosphere of the Royal Flying Corps, and one Intelligence Officer recalled that heated discussions would develop among pilots as to whether he was 'tainted' by carrying a spy, and whether he too would be treated as a spy and shot if he were caught.

Despite such misgivings, there does not appear to be a single case where a pilot was tried, condemned and executed for landing an agent, although there were instances of pilots being tried by the Germans on suspicion of espionage. In September 1915, to give one example, an unnamed French pilot and a Sergeant James J. Bach, an American volunteer serving with the French Flying Corps, were both captured by the enemy after landing agents, and they were both tried by court martial a month later. In each case, the verdict was 'not guilty' and the men were sent to PoW camp.[17]

17

A Royal Air Force officer, Lieutenant W.J. Buchanan, was not dealt with in quite such a correct manner when he was captured by Bulgarian troops after being landed behind enemy lines on a scouting mission in September 1918; although wearing full uniform, he was informed bluntly that he was to be shot as a spy. When he informed his captors that it was quite lawful to land a military scout in uniform behind enemy lines under international legislation, he was told that Bulgarian law did not recognize this fact. Nevertheless, the Bulgarians relented and sent Buchanan off to prison camp.[18]

As will be seen from the foregoing instances, the Allied flying services — and for that matter their German opponents too — had amassed considerable experience in clandestine air operations, involving both landing and pickup techniques, by the end of hostilities in November 1918, and all the belligerent countries possessed intelligence organizations which were extensive, if somewhat unwieldy in operation.

As far as Great Britain was concerned, the 1920s and 1930s saw a progressive decline in the strength and efficiency of the Intelligence services, particularly those responsible for the conduct of irregular and clandestine warfare of the kind conducted by Lieutenant-Colonel T.E. Lawrence in Arabia and by other, less famous officers on a smaller scale on India's North-West Frontier in the turbulent years that followed the end of the First World War. It was not until the spring of 1938, after Hitler's annexation of Austria brought the possibility of an armed conflict in Europe a few steps closer, that official British interest in clandestine operations was re-awakened, and three separate organizations were set up to investigate the possibility of subversive activities behind enemy lines in the event of another war.

The first, created in March 1938 as an internal department of the Foreign Office, was known simply as 'EH' and had its headquarters in Electra House on the Thames embankment. It was headed by Sir Campbell Stuart, who had been a prominent figure in the dissemination of propaganda to the enemy during the 1914-18 War; eventually, it was to be greatly expanded and re-designated the Political Warfare Executive.

The second department, also under Foreign Office authority, was known as 'Section D', and its brief was 'To investigate every possibility of attacking potential enemies by means other than the operations of military forces' — which, for practical purposes, meant building up a dossier of targets in Germany which were vulnerable to sabotage.

The third body was an integral part of the War Office and was known as GS(R), an abbreviation of General Staff — Research. Its personnel in the early days consisted of a solitary staff officer (who reported directly to the Vice Chief of the Imperial General Staff) and a typist. In the autumn of 1938, the staff officer responsible for GS(R) was an Engineer major named J.C.F. Holland, who had been placed in the post to recuperate following a bout of severe ill-health. Ironically, no more suitable man could have been found for the task. Holland had done a considerable amount of flying in the Middle East in 1917-18 and was consequently well aware of the potential of aircraft as an aid to conducting clandestine operations; he had also had much first-hand experience of terrorist activities in Ireland during the 1920s, and had made a close study of guerrilla warfare tactics in China and Spain.

Holland formed a close liaison with L.D. Grand, the head of Section D, and the two quickly worked out a system to avoid wasteful overlapping of activities. Both men forcefully put forward the case for the rapid preparation of methods for undertaking irregular operations of all kinds, and in March 1939 they finally made some headway; in conditions of the strictest secrecy, approval was given by a committee chaired by Lord Halifax, the Foreign Secretary, for active steps to be taken in setting up some sort of machinery for clandestine activities in countries which had already fallen under Nazi domination, or which were plainly threatened.

In the spring of 1939, soon after this decision, GS(R) was expanded slightly and re-designated MI(R), being now absorbed into the Military Intelligence Directorate. The latter was one of the four secret intelligence organizations that existed in Britain at this time; the others were the Secret Intelligence Service, also known as MI6, the Security Service, or MI5, and the Naval Intelligence Division.

Holland was joined by a new staff officer, Major Colin McVeagh Gubbins, an immaculate Scot who had seen action in Russia against the Bolsheviks in 1919 and who had also, like

19

Holland, fought against guerrillas in Ireland. Holland and his new companion were both firmly convinced that a European war was imminent, and in the summer of 1939, in conjunction with Section D, they discreetly assembled a nucleus of selected civilian volunteers — linguists, mountaineers, men with foreign business contacts or relevant specialist skills — and put them through a series of training courses in guerrilla tactics. During this period, Gubbins also made two secret journeys by air, one down the Danube Valley and one to Poland and the Baltic States, to investigate the possibility of setting up guerrilla activities among Germany's eastern neighbours.

During the period of the 'Phoney War', from September 1939 to April 1940, Holland and Gubbins initiated several enterprising schemes, two of which were later to bear much fruit: an escape network in western Europe and the Commandos. Gubbins, in fact, took an embryo Commando force to Norway in May 1940 and fought a brilliant rearguard action against the advancing Germans; it had no influence on the outcome of the campaign and was little more than a pinprick, but it was a foretaste of greater things to come. Apart from this, MI(R) appears to have carried out only one other commando-type activity during the period of the German *Blitzkrieg*; a reconnaissance by three Army officers who were landed on the French coast on the night of 2/3 June 1940. They blew up nearly a quarter of a million tons of oil in a French storage depot at Harfleur and returned home in a rowing boat on the 10th.[19]

During this period, MI(R) had tended to concentrate on establishing intelligence contacts in Poland and Czecho-slovakia, while Section D's main area of operations was France. Before the collapse, with the assistance of the Deuxième Bureau, Section D set up ten small caches of arms and explosives at various points in northern France between Rouen and Chalons-sur-Marne, each looked after by two French volunteers. Unfortunately, the Frenchmen were left with no clear instructions on how to go about sabotage activities under enemy occupation and so the stores were never used for their intended purpose, although some of the Frenchmen concerned later rendered invaluable service as members of escape lines.

By 25 May 1940, with the British Expeditionary Force pulling back towards the Dunkirk perimeter, the Dutch and Belgian armies shattered and the French under heavy pressure, it was clear that the early collapse of France — although not yet inevitable at this stage — was a growing possibility. On that date, the chiefs of staff advised the British War Cabinet — now headed by Winston Churchill — that even if Britain's European allies were overwhelmed, Germany 'might still be defeated by economic pressure, by a combination of air attack on economic objectives in Germany and on German morale and the creation of widespread revolt in her conquered territories'. To stimulate such a revolt, the chiefs of staff added, was 'of the very highest importance. A special organization will be required, and plans ... should be prepared, and all the necessary preparations and training should be proceeded with as a matter of urgency.'

A fortnight later, there was no longer any doubt that Britain would have to stand and fight alone, and the process leading to the establishment of a single organization to co-ordinate and control clandestine activities now gathered momentum, fired by Churchill's enthusiasm. Following a series of preliminary meetings in June, the decision that such an organization should be formed without delay was taken on 1 July, and on 16 July Churchill invited Hugh Dalton, the Minister of Economic Warfare, to take charge of all subversive activities. With his typical flair for the dramatic, Churchill's directive was to 'set Europe ablaze'.

The new organization was to be known as the Special Operations Executive. The detailed planning behind its creation was undertaken by Neville Chamberlain, Churchill's much-criticized predecessor; it was to be the last vital task he performed for the country he loved and had tried so hard to shield from another war, for a few days later he entered hospital suffering from the illness that was to end only with his death in November.

Although Dalton was to be the political head of SOE — responsible for keeping the chiefs of staff informed in general terms of his plans and in return receiving from them the broad strategic picture at regular intervals — its operational control was vested in Sir Frank Nelson, a former soldier and politician who had spent the early months of the war as British consul at

Berne, Switzerland. His real identity was disguised under the initials CD. His second in command was Sir Charles Hambro, a former Coldstream Guards officer and a prominent merchant banker, who eventually succeeded Nelson when the latter's health broke down in 1942. A third vital member of the SOE team was Colin Gubbins, now a brigadier and recipient of the DSO for his activities in Norway, who joined the organization in November 1940 (after much inter-departmental wrangling) and who in turn was to replace Hambro as CD in 1943.

SOE's original premises consisted of three dingy rooms in St Ermin's Hotel, Caxton Street, but in October 1940 the organization moved into much larger and airier accommodation at No. 64 Baker Street, and before long other buildings in the neighbourhood were also requisitioned.

Meanwhile, as SOE continued its endeavours to build up a nucleus of trained personnel to undertake subversive activities in the occupied territories, its directors found themselves having to fight hard to obtain even a small allocation of aircraft to deliver agents into the field. In the summer of 1940 the production lines of Britain's aircraft industry were working flat out to meet operational requirements and replace the considerable losses — particularly in bombers — suffered during the Battle of France, and aircraft were at a premium. Besides, only two types — the Armstrong Whitworth Whitley and the Vickers Wellington — were suitable for long-range parachute dropping operations. The RAF commanders mistrusted SOE, not least because of the aura of secrecy that surrounded it; as Sir Charles Portal, C-in-C Bomber Command during the early part of the war, remarked to an SOE officer:

> Your work is a gamble which may give us a valuable dividend or may produce nothing. It is anybody's guess. My bombing offensive is not a gamble. Its dividend is certain; it is a gilt-edged investment. I cannot divert aircraft from a certainty to a gamble which may be a gold-mine or may be completely worthless.

In fact, the only aircraft that could readily be spared to assist SOE operations in the summer of 1940 was the Westland Lysander Army co-operation monoplane. Several Army co-operation squadrons had been equipped with this type in France and production had been going ahead at a fast rate, but the Lysander had proved to be highly vulnerable to enemy fighters and some thirty had been lost before the end of the campaign in Flanders. In the desperate atmosphere of the time four new Lysander squadrons had been formed at home in July 1940 to help counter the anticipated German invasion and considerable numbers were shipped out to the Middle East, but it was becoming clear that the aircraft's intended role would soon have to be taken over by high-speed tactical reconnaissance aircraft and fighter-bombers. The Air Ministry therefore agreed to release a small number of Lysanders for special duties, although they would have to be shared by both the SOE and SIS (the Secret Intelligence Service). A number of Whitley Mk.V aircraft would also be allocated as and when they became available, although it was also emphasized that the latter would have to be made available for main force bombing operations as required.

It was a beginning; but for a year, up to August 1941, no more than five aircraft would be available for clandestine operations. In the early days, with the organization still gearing itself up and its hard core of agents still undergoing their rigorous training, it was just sufficient. It is doubtful whether, in 1940, even the most ardent supporter of SOE could have envisaged how the organization would burgeon as the war progressed, or foretell just how vast a role the Royal Air Force — and, later, the USAAF — would have to play in the infiltration and supply of its operatives.

PART ONE

Special Duties Air Operations from the
United Kingdom, 1940-45

1

The Early Days: The Special Duty Flight and No. 138 Squadron, 1940-41

The first Royal Air Force unit specifically designated for operations on behalf of SOE, No. 419 Flight, was formed at RAF North Weald, an important sector station in No. 11 Group, Fighter Command, on 21 August 1940. The Flight's commanding officer was Flight Lieutenant W.R. Farley, and its initial allocation of aircraft was two Lysanders, with two more in reserve.*

Working up to operational status was not easy, for North Weald was at that time receiving a lot of attention from the Luftwaffe, and early in September No. 419 Flight was transferred to a grass airfield at Stapleford Tawney, a few miles further south. Another move followed on 9 October, this time to Stradishall in Suffolk, and now two Armstrong Whitworth Whitley aircraft, with a third in reserve, were added to the Flight's inventory. Released by Bomber Command for special duties, these machines had been modified to drop parachutists and equipment by the provision of a simple hole in the fuselage floor. The Whitley was a slow, ponderous aircraft with definite limitations, such as a complete inability to remain airborne on one engine with anything other than a light load, but it had a radius of action of over eight hundred miles, which meant that it could reach targets deep inside Occupied Europe.†

On the night of 19/20 October, 1940, Wally Farley carried out the first ever Lysander pickup on behalf of SIS. His

---

* For details of Special Duties Squadrons and flights, see Appendix 1.
† For details of aircraft employed on SD work, see Appendix 2.

destination was a field near Montigny, in France, and his task was to pick up an agent named Philip Schneidau, who had been parachuted in from a 419 Flight Whitley on the night of 9/10 October. Farley flew down to Tangmere for the operation. (Agents and crews waiting to depart on Lysander special operations were billeted in a small house, concealed by tall hedges and situated opposite Tangmere's main gates. It was simply known as 'The Cottage'.) After some delay caused by bad weather, he eventually touched down in France at 01.17 hours on the morning of 20 October. Picking up the waiting agent, he turned into wind and took off again, but as he was climbing away a bullet from some unseen enemy rifle smashed the compass between his knees.

For a while Farley was able to map-read, but then the Lysander entered dense cloud and the pilot, without a compass, had to rely on his instinct to keep the aircraft flying in what he hoped was the right direction. In the rear seat, Schneidau was miserably wet and frozen to the bone, for the cockpit canopy had been removed before the flight to facilitate his entry.

By 06.30, the Lysander's fuel tanks were indicating 'empty', yet by some miracle the aircraft went on flying. Twenty minutes later, through a break in the cloud, Farley and his passenger sighted some cliffs. As far as they knew, they might be anywhere between north Germany and Ireland, for they had no idea of their position. However, Farley had no alternative but to set the aircraft down, for at that moment the engine cut out, finally starved of fuel. The Lysander glided down and, although Farley did his utmost to land safely, the aircraft struck some posts which had been planted along the cliff-top and smashed itself to pieces. Fortunately, neither occupant was hurt. It turned out that they had crash-landed at Oban, on the west coast of Scotland, after wandering practically the whole length of the British Isles. They spent the day at nearby RAF Oban, a Coastal Command station — where they had some understandable difficulty in satisfying the authorities that they were not spies — and returned to Stradishall twenty-four hours later.

Soon after this incident Farley went on leave, and while visiting North Weald one day he 'borrowed' a Hurricane to take part in a dogfight that was raging overhead. During the engagement he was shot down, but escaped with a broken leg.

Nevertheless, his injuries effectively brought a halt to his flying activities for a time.

In March 1941, the number of the Special Duties Unit was changed from 419 to 1419 Flight, to avoid possible confusion with No. 419 Squadron, one of the Royal Canadian Air Force bomber units due to be formed in England later that year. The Flight also had a new commander, Squadron Leader E.V. ('Teddy') Knowles, DFC. Its equipment now consisted of two Lysanders, three Whitleys, and a solitary Martin Maryland bomber. The latter aircraft, originally intended for France, had been allocated to the Flight for trials, as it was thought that its relatively high speed (270 mph cruise, compared with the Whitley's 200 mph) would give it a higher chance of survival on long-range operations over Europe during the summer months, with their long hours of daylight. However, a number of technical snags emerged during trials with 1419 Flight, and the Maryland was eventually declared unsuitable.

On the night of 11/12 April, Flying Officer Gordon Scotter of 1419 Flight carried out the second Lysander pickup operation. The aircraft he flew was V9287, the first to be fitted with a 150-gallon long-range fuel tank and a permanently-fixed ladder leading up to the rear cockpit.

Scotter's objective was a field north of Châteauroux between Levroux and Brion, in Vichy France. On the outward trip from Tangmere he narrowly missed being intercepted by enemy night-fighters fitted with searchlights, and in throwing them off he lost his bearings for a while, but he eventually found the field and went in to land. The surface was very rough and a series of deep ruts almost wrecked the Lysander's undercarriage, but the aircraft's robust structure withstood the shock and Scotter, shaken but unharmed, taxied to where the reception committee was waiting. His agent clambered quickly aboard and his baggage was thrown into the cockpit after him. Scotter concluded that no time was to be lost and opened the throttle wide, using emergency boost to obtain more take-off power, and as he climbed away into the darkness he saw car headlights approaching the field. Whether it was the Vichy police closing in for the kill or not, he never discovered. Scotter crossed the Channel safely, but on reaching Tangmere he found that there was an air-raid alert in force, so the flarepath could not be lit. He cruised around for a while, and eventually landed without the aid of lights. For completing this operation successfully, Scotter was awarded the DFC.

The same pilot carried out another pickup on 10 May 1941, when he flew to Fontainebleau to collect Philip Schneidau, who had been dropped back into France from a 1419 Flight Whitley on 10 March. Scotter picked up Schneidau from a spot close to the latter's home and brought him safely back, despite the fact that he was once again chased by enemy night-fighters carrying searchlights.

No. 1419 Flight's small force of Whitleys was active throughout the spring and summer of 1941, taking full advantage of fine weather and a full moon. The April-June period, however, got away to a bad start when one of the Flight's Whitleys — the only one modified to drop supply containers — set off from Tangmere on the night of 10/11 April with the task of dropping six Polish SOE saboteurs and their equipment to attack the Pessac power station at Merignac. An electrical short-circuit resulted in the two supply containers dropping away over the lower Loire, and the crew had no choice but to turn back. Unfortunately, the Whitley crashed on landing at Tangmere, killing or injuring all the agents and crew.

May was a better month, with several operations flown during the first fortnight. On the night of 5/6 May, SOE operative Georges Begue was dropped blind, with no reception waiting, into unoccupied central France, about twenty miles north of Châteauroux; on 10/11 May Pierre de Vomecourt parachuted into the same area, to be followed by Roger Cottin three nights later; and on 11/12 May a Whitley dropped three French agents named Forman, Varnier and Cabbard near Bordeaux, together with a container, again on a mission to destroy a power station. On the night of 12/13 June, another Whitley dropped two supply containers close to de Vomecourt's chateau at Bas Soleil, ten miles east of Limoges; these were retrieved by de Vomecourt and his gardener and their contents hidden for future use.

On 22 May 1941 No. 1419 Flight moved to a new base at Newmarket. All flying was done from the great grass expanse of Newmarket Heath, which provided the heavily-laden Whitleys with a good take-off run, and the crews were billeted in the racecourse grandstand until a proper mess could be arranged in Sefton Lodge, which was a training establishment in Newmarket itself.

The move brought a new kind of professionalism to the whole spectrum of special duties operations, with far closer liaison than had hitherto been the case between the RAF and SOE. One of the tasks allocated to the pilots of 1419 Flight was to train SOE operatives in selecting a suitable field and laying out an adequate flarepath, as well as in correct signalling procedures. The entire process was rehearsed exhaustively, the Lysander pilots and the agents practising simulated drops and pickups in selected fields dotted around the flat Cambridgeshire countryside. Lysander pilots were also encouraged to fly on operational Whitley sorties, to gain experience of all kinds of operating conditions over occupied Europe. On 25 August 1941, No. 1419 Flight became No. 138 Squadron. It was still commanded by Teddy Knowles, who had now been promoted to Wing Commander; his two flight commanders were Squadron Leader A.D. Jackson ('A' Flight, Whitleys) and Squadron Leader John Nesbitt-Dufort, DSO ('B' Flight, Lysanders). The latter had been an RAF officer since 1930, and was a highly experienced pilot. He had the curious nickname of 'Whippy', which had stuck with him since the day when, as a trainee fighter pilot, he had misjudged a camera-gun attack during an air exercise and flown slap through the middle of two formations of Hawker Fury and Hawker Hart biplanes, scattering them across the sky. Back on the ground, his furious squadron commander had roared at him, 'Where the bloody hell did you think you were, anyway? Whipsnade Zoo?' And 'Whippy' it had been thereafter.

No. 138 Squadron's complement of aircraft consisted of eight Whitleys, with two more in reserve, the solitary Maryland, two four-engined Handley Page Halifax II bombers (the latter undergoing trials to assess their suitability for special operations) and one Lysander. The Maryland was eventually replaced by a Wellington in October.

The Squadron's first operational sortie was flown on the night of 29/30 August, when a Whitley captained by Flying Officer Ron Hockey, with Squadron Leader P.C. Pickard as co-pilot, carried out Operation Trombone, dropping an electrical-engineer called Lencement near Châteauroux at 23.42 hours. (Lencement had instructions to form three Resistance circuits, but was arrested before the end of the year. He spent the rest of the war in various prisons and concentration camps, but somehow survived.) The drop was made from a height of 500 feet and the Whitley returned to base at 03.56 hours.

The first Lysander pickup operation by 138 Squadron was flown by John Nesbitt-Dufort on the night of 4/5 September 1941, operating out of Tangmere. The Lysanders were to operate out of this Sussex airfield as a matter of routine, to extend their radius of action, whereas the Whitleys flew from their home base at Newmarket. Generally, the procedure was that the Lysander pilot would fly down to Tangmere in the morning, sleep in the afternoon and then have a good meal in the evening, followed by a thorough briefing. Usually, the selected field in occupied territory had been photographed earlier by a high-flying Spitfire of the RAF Photographic Reconnaissance Unit, and this was of enormous value to the pickup pilot in selecting nearby landmarks.

Nesbitt-Dufort took off on his first pickup sortie at 23.00, carrying an SOE agent named Gerry Morel, and set course for Châteauroux via Tours, finding a flashing beacon at the latter location — which the Germans inexplicably continued to operate during the first two years of the Occupation — an invaluable aid to navigation. He located the target field without serious difficulty, and on time, but there were no visual signals. After circling for a quarter of an hour, he had just made up his mind to turn for home when he saw the letter 'G' — the correct recognition signal — being flashed to him in morse from a field some distance away from the designated one.

The pilot turned in for a landing, which he accomplished successfully, but to his dismay found that the field was much too small for what he considered a safe take-off. Nevertheless, he had no option but to try. Disembarking Morel, he took on another agent, Jacques de Guélis, and turned into wind, opening up to full boost. Not only was the field too small — a line of trees ran across the far boundary, right in the Lysander's take-off path. There could be no question of holding the aircraft down for a few seconds to gain safe flying speed. Nesbitt-Dufort hauled her off the ground and almost stood her on her tail, with the engine screaming at full power. Somehow he missed the trees, but there was a sudden blinding flash as his undercarriage sliced through some high-tension cables he had failed to see. The aircraft lurched but stayed in the air, and a second later its propeller churned through some telephone wires. Then the danger was over, and the pilot allowed the speed to build up before easing round on a climbing turn in the direction of home.

Nesbitt-Dufort reached the French coast ninety minutes later. There was no flak, which was unusual, and a moment later he discovered the reason for its absence. Converging on him, from the port side, he saw two green lights which could only be the navigational wingtip lights of enemy night-fighters. The Lysander pilot went into a steep diving turn to the left, passing below the pursuers; as he later pointed out, if he had turned to the right the enemy pilots would almost certainly have seen the foot-long blue flames from the Lysander's exhausts. The Lysander pilot maintained his new heading for a while, then turned to port, heading back into France once more. After a few minutes, Nesbitt-Dufort saw the lights of the enemy fighters receding in the distance, so he turned and headed out towards the Channel once more, pushing down the nose and opening the throttle. He streaked low over the sea until he was certain that he was not being followed, then climbed back to 2,000 feet and switched on his IFF (Identification Friend or Foe) device, a transponder that informed friendly radars that his was a friendly aircraft.

His radio failed on the approach to Tangmere, and there was a thick ground mist, but the Lysander had been picked up and identified by radar and a cone of searchlights around Portsmouth helped him home in on the airfield. Nesbitt-Dufort later discovered the reason why the field in France was not the designated one; de Guélis and his helper had been stopped en route for a routine papers check, and as they approached the pickup area they had heard Nesbitt-Dufort's Lysander circling overhead. Accordingly, they had gone into the nearest field and laid out the flarepath, fearing that the police might be close behind them, and that the Lysander might leave without them — as indeed it would have done, but for their prompt action.

Nesbitt-Dufort had another hair-raising experience on the night of 9/10 September, when he accompanied Flying Officer

Ron Hockey in Whitley T4166 to drop an agent deep inside occupied France. The drop was made successfully, but as the Whitley approached the French coast on the homeward run it emerged from cloud cover into brilliant moonlight. To get clear of light flak, Hockey took the aircraft in a long climb to 14,000 feet over the Franco-Belgian border, but four miles south of Ostend the blue beam of a radar-controlled German master searchlight fastened on it. Almost immediately, the Whitley was coned by a dozen searchlights, trapped like a fly in a spider's web, and the flak started to come up.

Hockey had just begun to take evasive action when a terrific explosion under the tail stood the Whitley on its nose and it went into a dive that was almost vertical. With the needle of the airspeed indicator 'off the clock' and the altimeter unwinding with terrifying speed, it took the combined efforts of Hockey and Nesbitt-Dufort, pulling back on the dual control columns, to bring the machine out of its headlong plunge. Both pilots had their feet braced against the instrument panel and were heaving with all their might. When the Whitley came shuddering out of the dive at just over a thousand feet, the crew blacked out momentarily with the tremendous 'g' force. When they could see again, the pilots found that the aircraft was flying straight and level only 400 feet above the sea, with the flak and searchlights behind it.

Hockey took the aircraft up to 4,000 feet as the English coastline drew closer, and the crew began to relax, but their troubles were by no means over. As the Whitley approached Harwich, it was subjected to a terrific barrage from the multiple pom-poms of some Royal Navy destroyers, whose gunners evidently mistook it for an enemy machine. Nesbitt-Dufort hastily opened the clear vision panel in the side of the cockpit and fired off the colours of the day, whereupon the anti-aircraft fire stopped.

Then came the last straw; the wireless operator told the pilots that East Anglia was covered in fog, which meant that there was no chance of landing at either Newmarket or Stradishall. Hockey set course northwards for Waddington, in Lincolnshire, but the weather closed in there as well, as it did over the Yorkshire airfield of Driffield. Eventually, at 07.00 on 10 September, nine hours after it had first taken off, the Whitley touched down at Leuchars, in Scotland.[20]

September 1941 saw a change in the composition of No. 138 Squadron's personnel. Hitherto, all aircrew for the Squadron (and for 1419 Flight before it) had been drawn from RAF personnel, but in September, following a request from the Polish leader in exile, General Sikorski, permission was granted for three Polish bomber crews to be attached to the unit. The reason for this was that a programme of long-range flights to Poland was being planned for the coming months, and as a political gesture it was felt appropriate that at least some of these should be undertaken by Polish airmen.

An experimental deep-penetration flight to Poland had, in fact, already been carried out earlier in the year by the former 419 Flight. In December 1940, plans had been laid for a Whitley to drop three agents in Polish territory, and they had been about to board the aircraft at Stradishall on the 21st when the mission had been cancelled because strong headwinds were forecast for the return flight. A second attempt was made in January 1941, and this time everything went smoothly. After an uneventful flight over snow-covered Europe, via the northern tip of Denmark and Bornholm Island, the Whitley dropped three agents in German territory close to the pre-war frontier at Bielsko. Unfortunately, the party lost all its equipment, and one of the agents injured his legs severely during the landing. However, the mission did much to bolster the morale of the Polish government in exile, and the team of agents was the first of many more which were to follow over the next four years; years during which No. 138 Squadron was to form a very special relationship indeed with the Poles.

The night of 1/2 October saw Squadron Leader Nesbitt-Dufort involved in another Lysander pickup operation, flying to a field at Estrées-St-Denis, not far from Compiegne, to pick up an agent known by the code-names of 'Armand' and 'Valentin'. He was in fact Captain Roman Czerniawski of the Polish Air Force, a gallant man who, following the dismembering of Poland in 1939, had escaped to France to carry on the fight as a pilot in the Armée de l'Air. On France's defeat, he had stayed behind to help set up the Resistance network. The pickup operation, code-named 'Brick', was completely successful, the Lysander spending only three minutes on the ground.

On 29 October 1941, two of 138 Squadron's Whitleys — Z9158 (Squadron Leader Jackson) and Z9159 (Pilot Officer Austin) took off for Portreath on the first leg of a flight to Malta, where the two aircraft were to be based for a special operation involving the dropping of agents and containers into Yugoslavia. They landed at Portreath at 13.30 hours in a gale, and were unable to proceed further that day because of adverse weather conditions over France and some unserviceability problems. The following day was spent in check-swinging the D/F loops of both aircraft and in route planning, but once again severe icing conditions over France kept the Whitleys on the ground.

Weather conditions were still poor on the last day of the month, but at 08.30 on 1 November the two aircraft were finally authorized to fly the next leg of the journey, to Gibraltar. They arrived there at 16.30, refuelled, and took off for Malta at 21.00, eventually reaching the besieged island at 05.00 on 2 November. An air raid was in progress when they landed at Luqa, but the aircraft were quickly dispersed and suffered no damage. Three Wellingtons also arrived shortly afterwards, although these had nothing to do with 138's operation, and to the battered and weary personnel at Luqa it must have seemed that the five bombers were the vanguard of a larger force which had come to the island to strike back at the enemy. The Whitley crews were certainly plied with questions, which they persistently refused to answer, about the purpose of their visit, until they reached the point when it would have come as a welcome break to go off and bomb some target in Italy or Sicily; but they were under the specific orders of the Directorate of Intelligence to engage in no operation other than that for which they had come to Malta, so they were grounded in frustration for a week.

Finally, on the night of 7 November, a submarine arrived in Grand Harbour carrying the equipment the Whitleys were to drop in Yugoslavia and also a Major McKenzie, who was in charge of the army side of the operation. That same night, a flying boat brought in more equipment, together with two Serbian pilots who knew the mountainous terrain of Yugoslavia intimately. At a conference the following day, held in the office of the Senior Air Staff Officer, Malta, it was decided after all the factors had been taken into consideration that night operations

36

over the mountains of Yugoslavia at this time of year would not be feasible, because of high winds and severe icing conditions, and consequently the drop would have to be made in daylight.

In the early hours of 9 November, Pilot Officer Austin took off carrying the two containers which had been made ready. With him in the Whitley was one of the Serbian pilots, to assist with navigation. The crew found the dropping zone without undue difficulty in daylight and the Whitley flew back to Malta after releasing the containers. No flak or fighters were encountered throughout the entire trip over enemy territory.

Two more agents arrived by submarine on the same day, but they had no parachutes with them and there were no spares to be had on Malta, so a planned drop on the night of 10/11 November had to be cancelled. Matters were further complicated by the fact that Squadron Leader Jackson's Whitley was unserviceable. In the end, a signal was received from the Air Ministry calling off the whole operation and ordering the two aircraft to return to England. Inclement weather delayed the return trip until 17.00 hours on 15 November, when the two aircraft finally took off on their homeward flight. After a brief refuelling stop in Gibraltar, the Whitleys reached home at 04.30 the next morning, Austin landing at West Malling and Jackson at Newmarket.[21]

November 1941 saw Wing Commander Knowles, No. 138 Squadron's commanding officer, posted away from the unit to take up a new appointment. (He was posted to command RAF Jurby in the Isle of Man, and was accidentally killed later while flying a Whitley.) Knowles had done a magnificent job in seeing the Special Duties Squadron through its formative months; his place was now taken by Wally Farley, who was promoted to Wing Commander and who was finally returning to operations after recovering from the injuries he had received after being shot down a year earlier. Sadly, the Squadron's record during this period was marred by the loss of three Whitleys and their crews, all of them in flying accidents. There was one pickup operation in November, flown by Squadron Leader Nesbitt-Dufort on the night of 7/8. The exact location is not recorded, but he returned with two agents.

There was one pickup operation the next month, too, on the night of 8/9 December. This was undertaken by a new pickup pilot, Flight Lieutenant A.M. ('Sticky') Murphy, and very nearly ended in disaster. Carrying one passenger, he found his objective — a field near Neufchâteau, in Belgium — without trouble, but to his consternation the visual signals flashed at him from the ground were incorrect. Breaking all the rules, Murphy went ahead and landed, but as a precaution he touched down well clear of the flarepath. As he taxied the Lysander cautiously towards the first torch, he switched on his landing light — and the beam lit up what seemed to be enemy troops.

Wasting no time, Murphy swung his aircraft round and opened the throttle wide, coming under heavy fire as he took off. He sensed the Lysander shudder as it was hit several times, and felt a stinging pain in his neck just as the wheels left the ground. Turning steeply to avoid a line of trees he headed away from the scene at low level, and although weak from loss of blood he managed to bring the bullet-riddled machine safely home. Later, the ground crew counted over thirty holes in it, and the pilot himself had been extremely lucky; a bullet had passed right through his neck without causing serious damage.

On 18 December 1941 the Squadron moved to Stradishall, the former base of the old 1419 Flight. No. 138's equipment at this date was twelve Whitley Mk.Vs, three Halifaxes and three Lysanders (serial numbers of the latter were T1508, T1771 and R2626).

During the last three months of 1941, the Halifaxes were used on a number of long-range sorties to Czechoslovakia. The first of these flights which is on record was flown on 3/4 October, when a 138 Squadron Halifax undertook Operation 'Percentage', a joint air drop and bombing operation. With the agents and 1,100 gallons of fuel on board, the aircraft took off at 19.10 on the 3rd, piloted by Flying Officer Ron Hockey, and set course for Prague across the heart of occupied Europe. The southern suburbs of Prague were sighted through a thick ground haze at 00.35, and after negotiating some inaccurate flak Hockey picked up the River Elbe near Kolin. There was some accurate flak here, and searchlights, but Hockey avoided them and flew down the Elbe in poor visibility. Pardubice was reached at 01.03 hours, the Halifax flying at 3,000 feet, and Hockey turned southwards for the target area. Although no visual signals were seen it was decided to go ahead with the operation, and two agents parachuted down. On the return flight, Hockey dropped his bombs through a gap in the cloud on a railway line near Hochstadt, the rear gunner reporting bursts and fires. Some more flak and searchlights were encountered on the return flight, but the aircraft landed safely at Tangmere in bad weather at 06.35.

Hockey made another trip to Czechoslovakia on the night of 28/29 December 1941, flying Halifax NF:V L9613, again from Tangmere. Over Germany, near Darmstadt, the crew sighted an enemy night-fighter, but although two flares were dropped by the latter it failed to intercept, which was just as well, for the Halifax was too heavily laden to take evasive action. As the Halifax flew on, it became impossible to take accurate fixes, for a heavy blanket of snow blotted out all landmarks such as roads and railway lines. However, at 02.12 flak was seen ahead, and the navigator identified its source as the town of Pilsen. Hockey altered course to the south of the town, heading for the target area. On this occasion the Halifax carried six agents, who were to be dropped in pairs on three separate targets, and although the latter could not be pinpointed the drops went ahead, the operation being completed by 02.46. The return flight was made via Pilsen and Darmstadt, but after the latter town the crew found it impossible, because of the snow, to identify any landmark until flak spat at them from the neighbourhood of Brussels. Hockey altered course westwards and crossed the coast at 07.20. Soon afterwards the transparent cockpit hood came loose and had to be held in place by the second pilot to prevent it from whirling back in the airflow and possibly damaging the tail, Hockey making his cold and thankless task easier by reducing the speed to 140 mph. The English coast was crossed near Selsey Bill and the Halifax landed at Tangmere at 08.19.

(Two of the agents dropped near Pilsen on this operation — Czech NCOs named Kubis and Gabchik — were later instrumental in the assassination of SS-Obergruppenführer Reinhard Heydrich, 'Protector' of Bohemia and Moravia and Himmler's right-hand man, on 27 May 1942. The killing led to a savage reprisal by the SS: the destruction of Lidice and the massacre of all its inhabitants.)

Long-range operations were severely hampered by bad weather during January 1942, and only one Lysander pickup was made during the month. This was Operation 'Beryl', flown on the night of 28/29 January by Squadron Leader Nesbitt-Dufort. His task was to fly to a field near Issoudun, south of the Loire, deliver one agent and pick up two more.

The outward trip was accomplished without incident; the agents were exchanged and the Lysander was soon on its way home. Soon afterwards, however, the pilot ran into trouble when dense cloud forced him further and further down until he was flying at only seventy feet, hedge-hopping in heavy rain. Then ice began to form on the windscreen and the leading edges of the wings. Realizing that it was hopeless to fly on in those conditions, Nesbitt-Dufort turned back into France, heading southwards until he reached the River Seine before turning once more on a course that would take him across the Channel to Beachy Head. This time he tried to get above the cloud, climbing to 8,000 feet through torrential rain. The icing, however, persisted, building up to a layer of three or four inches on the leading edges of the wings. The Lysander's engine began to run roughly, and although the pilot gave it full power the aircraft refused to climb any higher. As the icing grew worse the Lysander became almost uncontrollable, wallowing through the air and threatening to spin at any moment.

A minute later the aircraft began to lose height rapidly, and as they were now over the French coast again the pilot decided that the only thing to do was turn back into France and risk another landing. Diving to pick up speed, Nesbitt-Dufort brought the Lysander round until it was flying on a reciprocal course, and continued to dive until the airspeed indicator showed 240 mph. Ice crackled from the wings and propeller with a noise like machine-gun fire, and as more of it dropped off the aircraft became easier to control. At 2,500 feet the pilot eased out of the dive, descending cautiously through cloud until he broke through the base at 1,000 feet.

The Lysander was flying steadily now, but the huge cold front still barred its path to the north-west. It obscured the whole of the French coast from horizon to horizon, and Nesbitt-Dufort cruised backwards and forwards along it for more than a hundred miles, searching in vain for a break. With no chance of getting through and the aircraft rapidly running out of fuel, he decided to fly back to the field where he had made the original pickup and see if he could deliver his two agents safely back to their Resistance group. If he chanced a landing anywhere else, he reasoned, the odds were that they would all be captured.

He crossed the River Loire at Orleans and flew on south, heading for Châteauroux. A few miles south of the river, however, the Lysander ran out of fuel. Nesbitt-Dufort picked the likeliest-looking field and brought the aircraft down for a landing, but he failed to see a ditch than ran across his path. The Lysander's undercarriage went over the edge and there was a terrific crash as the machine came to rest on its nose, its tail sticking up in the air.

The three men staggered from the wreck with no worse injuries than a few cuts and bruises. All of them were exhausted by their ordeal in the storm, particularly Nesbitt-Dufort, who had spent seven hours at the controls. An hour after leaving the wreck he stumbled into a hut beside a road and fell fast asleep; nothing the agents could do would rouse him, so one of them decided to stay with him while the other went to get help from the nearest town. Luckily for all three, the French Resistance in this area was well organized, and it was not long before a car arrived to take the pilot and the other agent to a safe hiding place. Nesbitt-Dufort was to stay on the run for a month, before eventually being picked up by another aircraft from England, as we shall see later.

During his enforced absence, there were major changes in the organization of the RAF's special duties structure, the most important of which was the formation of a second SD squadron to specialize in pickups from the Continent. From now on, the crews of No. 138 would be the long-range specialists, their clandestine flights taking them to the farthest corners of occupied Europe.

2

No. 161 Squadron Operations, 1942

The second of the RAF's special duties units, No. 161 Squadron, began to form at Newmarket on 14 February 1942, and owed its existence in part at least to the temporary disbandment of the King's Flight. The latter's aircraft — a Percival Q6 and a Lockheed Hudson — had been very rarely used during 1941, and so the decision was taken to disband the Flight and absorb it, together with some of its personnel and one of its aircraft — the Hudson — into the new 161 Squadron.

The squadron's first commanding officer was Wing Commander E.H. 'Mouse' Fielden, MVO, AFC, who had been Captain of the King's Flight — a title which, since it was bestowed by the Court and not the RAF, he subsequently retained. His nickname, singularly inappropriate for a man of such flint-like character and courage, was also of royal origin, having been given to him by Edward, Prince of Wales, when Fielden was his personal pilot in 1929.

Fielden had a mixed collection of aircraft at his disposal. There were seven Lysanders, most of them handed over from 138 Squadron, five Whitley B.IVs and B.Vs, all of them some-what the worse for wear, two Wellington B.1Cs and the former King's Flight Hudson. The latter was a well-appointed machine, having an upholstered cabin, six parachute chairs and a large luggage compartment in the bomb bay. It was also armed with two .303 Browning machine guns in a Boulton Paul turret, and when the aircraft went to 161 Squadron so did its two wireless operator/air gunners, Sergeant H.R. Figg and Leading Aircraftman L.G.A. Reed. (This aircraft, serial number N7263, remained on 161 Squadron's inventory until 1 August 1944 when it was stricken off charge after hitting a building on landing at Tempsford.)

Fielden was fortunate in the aircrews assigned to him. Highly experienced for the most part, they included Guy Lockhart and 'Sticky' Murphy from 138 Squadron, and it was Murphy who flew 161's first pickup operation on the night of 27/28 February, 1942. Code-named 'Baccarat', the operation was flown from Tangmere, Murphy taking off at 21.45 in the evening of the 27th with one passenger, a young woman, on board his Lysander. He located his destination, a field near St Saens, with some difficulty, for the cloud base over France was down to a thousand feet with a horizontal visibility underneath of less than two miles, but succeeded in landing safely on receipt of a visual signal to disembark his passenger and take on two more for the return journey.

On 1 March Murphy was promoted to Squadron Leader and given command of 161 Squadron's Lysander Flight, an upgrading that coincided with the squadron's move to Gravely, in Huntingdonshire. There was no real time to settle into the new location before the squadron carried out its next two operations, both on the night of 1/2 March. The first was a Lysander pickup, with Flying Officer Guy Lockhart carrying out his first mission of this kind. He flew to the Cabourg area and successfully collected two agents, bringing them back to England without incident and landing at Tangmere. The second operation that night was a considerably more hair-raising affair. It was flown by Sticky Murphy, whose brief was to fly to Issoudun in unoccupied France and pick up John Nesbitt-Dufort, together with the three agents the latter had originally gone to collect in January, writing off his Lysander in the process.

The problem here was that a Lysander could not accommodate four passengers; the trip would have to be made by a twin-engined aircraft. The Hudson would have been ideal for the job, but the former King's Flight machine was undergoing an overhaul and was not available; in fact, for a variety of reasons it would not join the squadron until June. Wing Commander Fielden therefore approached the Bomber Command Operational Training Unit at Abingdon and asked to borrow an Anson. The CO of the OTU agreed readily, little dreaming the purpose for which the aircraft was intended. The Anson, painted bright yellow and bearing the serial number R3316, was flown to Gravely by a 161 Squadron crew. As soon as it arrived it was seized by the ground staff, who sprayed it all over with a coat of matt black paint.

The aircraft, carrying Murphy and a wireless operator, Pilot Officer Cossar, took off from Tangmere at 21.00 with a full load of fuel and set course for the River Loire, fixing their position over Cabourg and Tours en route. They sighted the river at 23.15, but spent the next forty-five minutes lost in dense cloud and heavy rain before getting another pinpoint and regaining their heading for Issoudun.

On the pickup field, Nesbitt-Dufort waited anxiously with the three agents. At about 23.45 they heard the sound of aero-engines and grabbed their torches, flashing the pre-arranged signal. A few moments later, an aircraft roared low overhead; Nesbitt-Dufort thought that it looked like a Whitley bomber. In any event, it continued unswervingly on its course and vanished in the darkness. The four men continued their vigil. By midnight they were numb with cold, and there was still no sign of the promised pickup aircraft. The latter was now considerably overdue, and Nesbitt-Dufort was approached by the agents with a view to abandoning operations. The RAF pilot, however, refused to give up, and after some discussion persuaded the others to stay with him.

Minutes later — at 00.15, to be exact — they heard the roar of aero-engines yet again. At once, Nesbitt-Dufort recognized the distinctive note of an Avro Anson's Armstrong Siddeley Cheetah engines and at first could not believe his ears, for a 'twin' had never before been used for a pickup. But an Anson it was, sliding down from the northern sky. Once again, Nesbitt-Dufort and the agents flashed the recognition signals, and this time they were rewarded by answering lights from the aircraft. The Anson circled the field, its engines coughing as Murphy throttled back on the approach, and a few moments later its undercarriage bumped and rumbled over the grass surface. The Anson taxied in, the side window of the cockpit opened and Nesbitt-Dufort was greeted by a stream of cheerful invective.

'I thought it might be you, Sticky,' he yelled, to be answered by a shout of 'Get on board — we haven't much time!'

Cossar opened the hatch and the four men scrambled into the fuselage. Wasting no time, Murphy turned into wind and opened the throttles, sending the Anson lurching over the soggy ground. The take-off run seemed endless, but with the edge of the field looming up Murphy succeeded in lifting the aircraft off the ground at a speed later described by Nesbitt-Dufort as 'a steady trot'. Somehow, the pilot maintained flying speed and set course homewards, skirting the heavy flak defences of Dieppe and making an eventual safe landing at Tangmere at 02.40.

The Anson was flown back to Abingdon the following day, accompanied by a 161 Squadron Lysander. The Anson crew parked the machine on the flight line, jumped into the Lysander and took off for Gravely before anyone had time to ask why the OTU's formerly spick-and-span yellow aircraft had suddenly become a shade of dirty black overnight.

The badinage between Nesbitt-Dufort and Murphy continued even down to the written reports of the night's operation. 'The skill of the pilot and navigator', Nesbitt-Dufort wrote, 'proved in this case to be exceptional, as we were only lost the majority of the way home, which only goes to prove!' Murphy's terse account ended with the sentence: 'The above laconic report marks the completion of a very stout effort by the pilot and navigator and the Cooks tourist passenger!'[22]

Bad weather in March brought a temporary halt to further operations, and it was not until the night of the 26/27 that the next Lysander pickup was carried out. Once again the pilot was Guy Lockhart, who flew from Tangmere to a field near Saumur with one passenger (Renault-Roulier, alias Rémy) and picked up two more, Christian Pineau and François Faure. The Lysander spent fifteen minutes bogged down in mud at its destination, and was freed only after some hard pushing by the reception committee and passengers.

On 8 April 1941 No. 161 Squadron moved from Gravely to Tempsford, a little way to the north of Sandy, in Bedfordshire. On the face of it, Tempsford was hardly an ideal location for clandestine operations, for the A1 Great North Road lay on one side of it and the main London-Edinburgh railway line on the other. Yet its very openness may have helped to preserve its secret identity, for few railway passengers can have taken much notice of the few decrepit-looking and obviously out-of-date aircraft they spotted from the windows of their carriages as they passed by. The villagers of nearby Tempsford eventually guessed, inevitably, that something unusual was going on, but there were never any recorded instances of careless talk. Evidence that Tempsford's secret was very well kept lies in the fact that although the Germans knew that the special duties aircraft were operating from a base some thirty miles north of London, they only once came near to finding it; that happened one night in the spring of 1943, when a lone German bomber flew over the airfield and dropped a string of flares across it. The anti-aircraft defences kept silent, not wishing to betray the well-camouflaged objective. The bomber circled for some time but the crew apparently saw nothing and flew away, dropping their bombs on a nearby nursery garden.

No. 138 Squadron had already moved to Tempsford on 14 March 1942, and the two squadrons were now to operate side-by-side (apart from detachments overseas by No. 138 from time to time) for the duration of clandestine operations in Europe. Generally, No. 138 was to be responsible for the parachuting of agents and supplies to long-range objectives, while No. 161 worked closer to home and, with its Lysanders, had the task of undertaking all pickup missions from occupied territory. During the spring and early summer of 1942, the Whitleys and Wellingtons of both units frequently joined other Bomber Command aircraft in attacking targets on the Continent.

Only one pickup was flown by No. 161 in April prior to its move to Tempsford, and that was on the first night of the month, when Squadron Leader Murphy flew to Les Andelys-sur-Seine with one agent and brought back two others. After that, partly due to the period of settling in at the Squadron's new location, it was nearly a month before the next such operation was carried out. Yet again the Lysander pilot was Guy Lockhart, who on the night of 26/27 April carried a Free French radio operator, Pierre Beech, to a landing field ten miles north-north-east of Châteauroux and almost came to grief.

The reception committee, as it turned out, had no real knowledge of how to lay out a flarepath, or even of the kind of ground that was suitable for a landing. As a result, they laid out their torches on a hill, and Lockhart, who was unaware of this, made a particularly heavy landing. For some unrecorded reason (possibly a small fuel spillage) the engine caught fire, so he hurriedly switched off and waited for the flames to die away. Meanwhile, his passenger climbed down from the cockpit and vanished in the darkness. After a few minutes the fire went out, and Lockhart managed to restart the engine. He taxied to the end of the flarepath, where the two men he was to pick up — Gaston Tavian and Capitaine de Vaisseau Mariotti — were waiting for him. He got them both on board and took off safely for England.

On the next night, 27/28 April, 'Sticky' Murphy also experienced trouble with his Lysander's Mercury engine during a sortie to a pickup field near St Saens. Taking off at 22.45, he tested his magneto switches over the coast at Beachy Head — as was the normal procedure on trips out of Tangmere — and the engine promptly cut out. He managed to get it started again, but it was running roughly so he returned to base. After some work by the ground crew, he took off once more at 00.45, eventually crossing the French coast some distance north of Le Treport. Navigation on this trip proved extremely difficult, because it was very dark under the cloud base and consequently landmarks were not easily distinguished. Nevertheless, the experienced Murphy succeeded in fixing his position at a point some fifteen miles north of St Saens, and at 02.00 he spotted the winking lights that identified his landing ground. He touched down and picked up two passengers, Resistance leaders Jacques Robert and Pierre Brossolette.

No. 161 Squadron's Operations Book records three pickup missions in May, all at the end of the month. Of two sorties flown on the night of 28/29 May, one was aborted when the pilot, Flight Lieutenant Lockhart (newly promoted at the beginning of the month) failed to locate any ground signals, and the second ended in disaster. The latter trip was flown by Flight Lieutenant John Mott, who took his Lysander to Le Grand Maleray, near Bourges in Vichy France, only to become hopelessly bogged down on landing. Mott and his passenger — Alex Nitelet, a former Belgian fighter pilot who, having suffered an eye injury during the Battle of France, had volunteered to work as a radio operator for SOE — made a run for it; Nitelet got away, but Mott was captured by the Vichy police and imprisoned. He subsequently escaped and found his way back to England via

Gibraltar, but never flew on clandestine operations again. His Lysander, which he had tried in vain to set on fire, was towed away by the Vichy police, but the vehicle towing it mysteriously broke down as it was being pulled over a level crossing seconds before the arrival of a fast train. The Lysander's demise was complete.

The third mission, flown by Squadron Leader Murphy the next night, was a success. This trip was also to unoccupied France, to a landing strip south of Vatan in fact, where Murphy successfully discharged two agents and took on two more. It was Murphy's last secret mission for SOE; a fortnight later he was posted elsewhere, sadly to be killed on operations later in the war. His place as OC Lysander Flight was taken by Guy Lockhart, who was now promoted to Acting Squadron Leader.

No pickup operations by 161 Squadron are recorded at all for June and July 1942, and on several occasions during this period the Lysanders joined the Squadron's Whitleys and Wellingtons in attacks on targets in France. These included the Oissel chemical factory, a power station at Aure and some rail yards. The Lysander's offensive load was small, consisting of a pair of 250-pound bombs attached to stub wings on the undercarriage fairings, but the aircraft's low speed and manoeuvrability enabled it to hit its target with a high degree of accuracy. In addition to Lockhart, pilots involved in these operations included Pilot Officers John Bridger and Peter Vaughan-Fowler, Flying Officer McIndoe, Flight Lieutenant Huntley and Warrant Officer Kingham. Air gunners were also carried.

The reason for the lengthy break from clandestine work was the treachery of a French woman agent, Mathilde Carré, known as 'The Cat', who for some time had been living with a sergeant in the German Abwehr, the field security police, and passing on vital information to him. Her activities resulted in the arrest of most of her colleagues, and for a time the SOE network in France was thrown into confusion.

The first recorded pickup by 161 Squadron after the long break came on the last night of August, when Guy Lockhart flew to a field in unoccupied France, near the Riviera, to collect Christian Pineau and another agent. Unfortunately, a faulty flarepath layout at his destination led to his aircraft running into a ditch and smashing its undercarriage, which left no alternative but to set fire to the machine. Fortunately, Lockhart learned that a pickup was shortly to be made by sea from a point on the Riviera, so he set off in that direction with the two agents. He did not know it at the time, but clandestine operations from Gibraltar to the south coast of France were a fairly common occurrence; they were carried out either by submarine, or by HMS *Fidelity*, a heavily-armed 1,500-ton merchant vessel, or more usually by a pair of twenty-ton feluccas crewed by Polish seamen under the command of two very brave lieutenants named Buchowski and Krajewski, both of whom were to earn DSOs in two years of hazardous work in this area.[23]

At the coast, just as they were about to board a dinghy to take them to the waiting felucca, Lockhart and his companions were intercepted by some Vichy coastguards, and shots were exchanged. Lockhart got away and reached the felucca, but the two agents fled inland and were later captured and imprisoned. Lockhart rejoined his unit on 13 September, and a few days later was awarded a DSO.

During September, several Lysander pickup sorties either had to be abandoned or were not completed because of bad weather. Peter Vaughan-Fowler and John Bridger both flew their first operations with the Squadron on the night of 25/26 September; Vaughan-Fowler failed to find his objective in the murk and returned to land at Exeter, while Bridger found his field all right near the junction of the rivers Ain and Rhône but sank his aircraft axle-deep in soft mud on landing. It was a stubble field and should not have been used at all — in fact that underlined the need for the proper training of reception committees in the layout of flarepaths on suitable ground — and to make matters worse the agents Bridger was to have collected had failed to turn up. Only after removing the side panels from his undercarriage spats and scraping mud from the wheels was Bridger able to take off, and even then it was touch and go. He returned to Tangmere utterly exhausted, after a round trip of nine and a half hours in the most appalling weather, carrying a solitary small package of mail. The bad weather conditions in September also probably contributed to the loss of two of the Squadron's Whitley aircraft, which went missing on operations during the month.

The first day of October saw the promotion of Wing

Commander Fielden to Group Captain, to command RAF Tempsford. He replaced Group Captain A.H. MacDonald, who had been OC Tempsford since February.

Fielden's replacement as OC 161 Squadron was Wing Commander Percy Pickard, a well-built, 26-year-old Yorkshireman from Sheffield who loathed his first name and was known to one and all simply as 'Pick'. He was something of a celebrity, having starred in a 1941 propaganda film about Bomber Command, 'Target for Tonight'. In May 1941 he had been appointed to command No. 9 Squadron, flying Vickers Wellingtons, and he led the first operational search for the German battle cruiser *Prinz Eugen*. By the autumn of that year he had flown 65 night operations, completing two tours.

His next command was No. 51 Squadron, equipped with Whitleys. On the night of 27/28 February 1942, in an historic mission known as Operation Biting, his squadron dropped a force of 119 men of the Parachute Regiment over Bruneval, near le Havre; their task was to dismantle and bring home vital parts of a top-secret German 'Wurzburg' radar installation. The raid was a complete success, the paratroops being evacuated by sea with their booty. By the time Pickard took command of 161 Squadron, his decorations consisted of a DSO and Bar, and a DFC. At this stage of the war, he was one of the most highly-decorated officers in the RAF.

October also saw the beginning of the end for 161 Squadron's venerable Whitleys, which from now on were progressively replaced by Handley Page Halifaxes. The first Halifax, a Mk.I (serial W1064) arrived at the end of September and was used for conversion to type; four Halifax Mk.Vs (DG244, DG245, DG285 and DG268) were added to the Squadron's inventory during October. Five Whitleys, however, continued to serve with the Squadron for a while longer; these were Mk.Vs BD363, BD267, BD223 and Z9438.

Two more new aircraft types joined the Squadron in October 1942. The first of these was the Armstrong Whitworth Albemarle, a twin-engined machine which had been designed as a medium bomber but which was never used in its intended role. Thirty-two Albemarle Mk.Is had been built, the first in December 1941, and 161 Squadron received two of this batch, P1378 and P1390. The other new type was the Douglas Havoc, the night-fighter/intruder version of the twin-engined Douglas Boston light bomber. It was an American aircraft, and those serving with the RAF had originally been intended for the French Air Force. Very few had been delivered before the French collapse in 1940, so the RAF, desperate for bombers of all kinds, received the balance. Two Havocs, BJ477 and AW399, were allocated to 161 Squadron. Together with the two Albemarles, they were detached to St Eval, in Cornwall, for special duties, as we shall see later.

Apart from this influx of material, October was remarkable only for its continual bad weather. Of six Lysander pickup attempts during the moon period that month, four had to be abandoned because of excessive cloud over the target areas. Two of the abandoned missions were flown by Pickard, the other two by Flying Officer R.G. McIndoe. John Bridger made a successful landing on the night of 26/27 October, dropping off SOE operative Mary Lindell in a field near Clermont-Ferrand, while Peter Vaughan-Fowler landed north of Mâcon to disembark two passengers, taking on two more for the return trip.

Despite more bad weather in November, most of 161 Squadron's Whitley and Lysander operations were successfully completed, although two Whitleys were lost during the month. One was hit by flak over the target area and crashed, but the crew baled out and were later reported to be prisoners of war; the other, engaged on a drop over southern France, had engine trouble over the Bay of Biscay and made for Portuguese territory, where it crash-landed.

The first Lysander pickup operation in November was flown by John Bridger on the night of the 17/18. After flying in and out of dense cloud for some time, he eventually located his target field at Courlaoux, four miles south-west of Lons-le-Saunier, and made a safe landing, dropping two agents and embarking two more.

On the following night, for the first time ever, a double Lysander sortie was flown to the same objective, a field fifteen miles north-north-east of Châteauroux. The pilots were Guy Lockhart and Peter Vaughan-Fowler. Unfortunately, because of the prevailing weather conditions, it proved impossible to locate the target, so the two Lysander pilots abandoned the operation and set course for home with their outbound agents still on board. Because of the weather conditions there was no question of making the trip at low level; instead, the Lysanders had to fly above a blanket of cloud, silhouetted like moths in the brilliant moonlight. For safety's sake, they followed different homeward headings.

Lockhart's troubles began over the French coast near St Malo, when searchlight beams stabbed up through a break in the clouds and coned his Lysander, followed by heavy anti-aircraft fire. Lockhart and his passenger experienced an unpleasant couple of minutes as the Lysander twisted and turned; then the flak died away astern and the aircraft set out over the Channel. Over Jersey, Lockhart began to relax. In a short time he would be landing at Tangmere and tucking into the traditional post-operation breakfast of bacon and eggs. He looked around, enjoying the calm tranquillity of the moonlight on the cloudscape below, and at that moment he saw the enemy fighters. There were two of them, fast Focke-Wulf 190s — normally day-fighters — arrowing down on his tail, and a third was turning steeply from the starboard quarter to cut off Lockhart's homeward escape route. Before the enemy could open fire, Lockhart acted, closing the throttle and pulling back the stick. The Lysander shuddered, stalled and fell away in a spin towards the shelter of the clouds below. The machine dropped into the opaque layer like a stone and Lockhart let her go on spinning for long seconds before applying stick and rudder to bring her out.

As he emerged from the cloud base, low over the Channel, he was horrified to see that the Focke-Wulfs were still with him and closing in for the kill. It was now that the Lysander's manoeuvrability paid off. Opening the throttle, Lockhart sent the aircraft towards the sea in a power dive, then pulled it up towards the clouds once more in a climb far steeper than anything the fighters could follow. This time he stayed in cloud cover until he was over the English coast, by which time the Focke-Wulfs had abandoned the pursuit and gone home.

A second double Lysander operation was attempted on the night of 22/23 November; the pilots involved were Pickard and Bridger, and the target a field five miles south of Vatan, in the Châteauroux area. Two agents were to be flown out, and three brought back. The two outbound agents travelled in Bridger's aircraft, which was also to carry two of the three scheduled for the return trip. Pickard could only take one, because on this flight he carried a second crew member, Pilot Officer James McCairns.

McCairns was a recent posting to the Squadron. He had flown Spitfires during the early part of the war, and in July 1941 had been shot down and taken prisoner. Together with a Belgian, he had managed to escape from PoW camp and make his way to Belgium, crossing the border in a blizzard in January 1942 and going into hiding with the Belgian Underground in Brussels. Eventually, after many adventures along the escape route through France, he reached Gibraltar in May 1942, and returned to England, joining 161 Squadron after a well-earned rest. In November 1942 he had yet to fly his first Lysander sortie into France; the trip with Pickard was for 'familiarization' purposes, which was a departure from the usual procedure. It may be that Pickard was worried about the new arrival's prowess, for McCairns had far less night-flying experience than the Squadron's other pilots.

Both Lysanders crossed the French coast at Cabourg, near Caen, as was the normal practice. It meant an hour-long haul over the Channel, but this way they avoided the worst of the enemy anti-aircraft defences. Bridger found the field without too much difficulty, but Pickard, with McCairns helping to navigate in the back seat, got lost in the target area, and it was purely by chance that they spotted the three winking lights of the flarepath below. Much relieved, Pickard went down to land just as Bridger was taking off, and both aircraft returned safely home with their agents.

McCairns flew his first solo sortie to France three nights later, on 25/26 November. His destination was a field some fourteen miles to the south of Bourges, and this time there were no navigational errors. He landed safely, if rather heavily — having forgotten to trim the aircraft properly in his eagerness to get down — and unloaded his two agents, taking on two more. It was one of the fastest pickups made so far by a 161 Squadron pilot, and apart from some inaccurate flak near Bourges the return flight was uneventful. Peter Vaughan-Fowler also carried out a Lysander mission that night, flying to Thalamy to pick up three Corsican police inspectors who had helped an SOE agent, Marie-Madeleine Fourcade, to escape from a Vichy prison shortly before.

McCairns and Vaughan-Fowler flew a double Lysander sortie on the night of 28/29 November, but only McCairns found the target, a field two miles north of Magny, near Rouen. Vaughan-Fowler, after circling the area for some time and failing to see the necessary visual signals, gave up and went home; McCairns was also lost for thirty minutes in the target area, but after a lengthy search he saw the lights and went straight in to land. The passengers he collected were agent Max Petit, his wife and two children, escaping from France following a tip-off that the Gestapo were on their trail. (In fact, the Gestapo raided their home the next day.) It was the first time that a 161 Lysander had carried four passengers. Persistent bad weather severely curtailed operations during December 1942, a month that saw 161 Squadron 'B' Flight fully re-equipped with their new Halifaxes. The Lysanders of 'A' Flight, meanwhile, were detached to Tangmere for most of the month, in order to take full advantage of any sudden break in the weather. It was not until the night of 17/18 December, however, that the month's first Lysander pickup was carried out. The pilot was Guy Lockhart and the destination Chavannes, near Bourges. On landing, with two passengers on board, the Lysander's tail struck an unseen cart track that ran across the landing strip, resulting in the jamming of both elevator and rudder. He managed to free the latter by breaking the bottom rudder struts, but the elevator remained firmly stuck in the up position, refusing to budge even when Lockhart asked six Frenchmen to stand on it.

Even though he realized that the damage might make his aircraft almost uncontrollable he decided to risk a take-off, and the two passengers he had come to collect put their complete trust in his ability. He took off with far less difficulty than he had anticipated, and found that the aircraft would climb steeply at full throttle — although, because of the position of the jammed elevator, nothing he could do would persuade it to fly straight and level. He had no alternative but to let it climb, until it reached a height at which he and his passengers could no longer tolerate the cold; then he closed the throttle and allowed the

Lysander to sink. It was a tribute to the aircraft's handling characteristics that it did not stall or spin, but just mushed its way down until the pilot opened the throttle again. So, alternatively climbing and descending, he flew back to Tangmere, where he made a safe if unconventional landing.

It was Lockhart's last successful sortie with 161 Squadron. He made another flight on 22 December, but had to abort because of atrocious weather. Shortly afterwards, he was posted out to Air Ministry Intelligence for a well-earned rest. He was killed later in the war, commanding a bomber squadron in No. 8 (Pathfinder) Group.

Two other Lysander sorties were flown on the night of 22 December: one by Flight Lieutenant John Bridger, which was abandoned because of fog in the target area, and the other by Wing Commander Pickard, who landed successfully in a field near Issoudun and exchanged his pair of passengers. A sortie on 23 December by Pilot Officer McCairns, was also abandoned through fog, as was a second flown by Squadron Leader Hugh Verity, who had joined the Squadron in November and had been appointed to command the Lysander Flight. He was making his first operational trip with No. 161; in the two years that followed, he was to become one of the most outstanding pickup pilots of them all.[24]

3

The Build-up: No. 138 Squadron Operations, 1942

On 14 March 1942, No. 138 Squadron moved to Tempsford to operate alongside No. 161, and during the remainder of the year a definite pattern of operations began to emerge, with long-range flights taking place in the autumn, winter and early spring when cover of darkness was sufficient to allow the aircraft to attain their objectives and regain base without an insupportable risk of interception. During the shorter nights the aircraft flew to Norway, France and the Low Countries, and also to Austria and Czechoslovakia.

The use of the four-engined Halifaxes made it possible to undertake flights as far as central Poland, the aircraft usually routing across Denmark to avoid the worst of the German anti-aircraft defences. These flights lasted between eleven and fourteen hours depending on the weather, and as the long-range trips always took place in the winter, autumn and spring the conditions could be decidedly adverse with heavy icing and snow, not to mention high winds that resulted in more than one aircraft having to ditch in the inhospitable North Sea on the return journey. To increase their range the aircraft were stripped of every unnecessary fitting, including seats and sometimes heating, which made the flight extremely uncomfortable for both crew and passengers.

To add to the problems, the dropping techniques in use at the time meant that operations had to be carried out under full-moon conditions, without which the navigator had very little hope of guiding the aircraft to its destination or of finding the dropping zone and the tiny pinpricks of light that indicated where the drop was to be received. Taking into account the moon's phases, this meant that No. 138 could take advantage of only forty operational nights over the whole twelve-month period, and even then operations often had to be cancelled because of bad weather.

However, special operations accounted for only part of 138 Squadron's activities during 1942. Although, like No. 161, it came under the direct control of the Chief of Air Staff, it nevertheless formed part of No. 3 (Bomber) Group, and consequently was often called upon to take part in that Group's normal operations. Apart from supporting the main force squadrons of Bomber Command in attacks on enemy targets during this period, the Squadron also carried out numerous 'Nickels', or leaflet-dropping trips. On the night of 20/21 April 1942, for example, Whitley 'K', piloted by Sergeant Wilde, dropped leaflets in the Bayeux area; unfortunately, on the return flight to base it crashed near Porton and burst into flames, only the rear gunner surviving.[25]

Whereas in 1941 agents had usually been dropped singly into occupied territory, in 1942 they would more often be dropped in pairs, a key SOE or SIS man parachuting down in the company of his radio operator, or 'pianist'. It would be the responsibility of these two to make contact with and recruit reliable men and women from the towns and villages in their operating area, so that a 'committee' could be formed to select suitable dropping zones for future air supply. The 'pianist' would make radio contact with London, passing coded details of the place where the supply drop was to be made: each such place was given a code-name, a recognition letter and also a simple identification message, which would be broadcast by the BBC on the day when the drop was due. The message, in fact, was broadcast twice, the first time at 13.00 hours and the second, by way of confirmation, at 18.00.

As soon as the 13.00 signal came through, the local reception committee would make their various ways to the dropping zone. This often involved a lengthy journey, complicated in winter by the imposition of a curfew at sunset, which meant that the Resistance worker whose task it was to follow on with the 18.00 confirmatory message might have to run the gauntlet of enemy patrols. It also meant that if no confirmation were forthcoming, the reception committee had to stay in the vicinity of the dropping zone until the curfew was lifted at sunrise, when they could make their way home. After spending a freezing night in the open or in some rudimentary shelter, the very effort of turning up for work the next day and appearing normal imposed a considerable physical and psychological strain.

For the RAF crews, accurate navigation to the target areas presented vast problems. In 1942, the radio-navigation aids that would one day be standard equipment in all bombers were still in the future; navigators had to rely on their maps, and on the accurate identification of ground features such as rivers, lakes and estuaries, which reflected the moonlight. It was a tribute to their skill and the high standard of their training that most of them did find their objectives, for their task was made even harder by the fact that all special duties sorties were flown at low level, enabling the aircraft to escape detection by losing itself in the clutter of return echoes from the ground that blotted part of the enemy's radar screens. It should be remembered that, in 1942, many bomber crews of the main force, flying at altitudes where accurate map-reading was a great deal easier, were failing to find their targets or to identify them properly.

As soon as they heard the noise of the incoming aircraft's engines, the reception committee would switch on the flarepath. This consisted of three or four torches in a straight line, with fifty metres between each one, and another offset to the right at the upwind end of the line, forming an inverted 'L'. Having sighted the lights, the pilot would make his run-in upwind, heading for the nearest light in the line, which would flash the identification code to him. If this was correct, he would make his drop from 500 feet if his load was containers, or 800 feet if a 'live' drop of agents was involved. Despite this relatively low altitude, the French section of SOE — to quote the only really reliable set of figures — suffered only six fatalities on operational parachute drops throughout the entire war, and of these, one occurred because his static line was not attached properly and another because his parachute had been improperly packed.

In dropping stores, two types of container were used, and these remained standard throughout the war. The first was the C Type, consisting of a single cylinder about six feet long and containing three cylindrical canisters, and the second was the H Type, comprising five separate cylindrical cells held together, during the drop, by a pair of metal rods. The latter was by far the more manageable of the two types, being easily broken down into its component parts for transport or concealment. A typical Halifax load of twelve containers would contain: 6 Bren light machine-guns, with 1,000 rounds of ammunition per gun, spare parts and 48 empty magazines; 36 .303 rifles with 150 rounds per gun; 27 Sten guns with 300 rounds per gun, 80 empty magazines and 16 loaders; 5 pistols (Smith and Wesson .38) with 50 rounds per gun; 40 Mills grenades and detonators; 12 Gammon grenades with 18 pounds of plastic explosive, fuse and adhesive tape; 156 field dressings; 6,600 rounds of 9-mm ammunition; 3,168 rounds of .303 ammunition; 20 empty Bren magazines and a similar number of empty Sten magazines. There were, of course, several variations on these loads, depending on the requirements of individual Resistance groups.[26]

Generally, the SOE operatives in the field had nothing but praise for the unknown men and women in England who packed their stores. Although accidents could and did happen — containers of grenades occasionally exploding on impact with the ground, for example — the vast majority of containers and their contents were delivered safely, and with far less loss than had been anticipated. (HQ SOE in London had estimated, when air supply started, that at least ten per cent of all stores dropped would fall into enemy hands.) On one occasion, two hundred glass bottles of printers' ink for an underground newspaper were dropped without a bottle being so much as cracked.

By the middle of 1942, the Halifaxes and Whitleys of 138 and 161 Squadrons were equipped with an item of radio equipment known as S-Phone, developed by SOE Signals Directorate and first tested in October 1940. S-Phone was a simple VHF transmitter/receiver, the master station — installed in the aircraft — being equipped with a 25-foot trailing aerial. It allowed two-way voice communication between the aircraft and an agent on the ground, and when it worked properly it had a range of about thirty miles. The snag was that the aircraft had to climb in order to pick up the ground signals, which was dangerous, as it could then be detected by enemy radar. Nevertheless, S-Phone did provide agents with the means of relaying coded messages speedily to SOE in London, and despite all its technical disadvantages it was the forerunner of much more sophisticated equipment that was to be used later in the war.

During the whole of 1942, 201 containers and 64 packages of various kinds were dropped into France alone by 138 and 161 Squadrons; the comparative figures for 1941 were 9 and 11. This total represented twenty-three tons of stores, delivered in ninety-three sorties, sometimes by one aircraft, sometimes more. In 1941, one and a half tons had been delivered in twenty-two sorties.

Many of the 64 packages dropped into France contained pigeons, and the 138 Squadron crews went to astonishing lengths to ensure that the birds had a safe drop, the pilots reducing speed to as little as 120 knots and releasing the packages from a greater height than was usual, to make sure that the parachutes deployed fully, and in general taking more care than they did when the drop involved a human being! The pigeons, tucked into little cages made out of cardboard material, were dropped from the exit hole on small parachutes, usually over a farm, village or some other spot where they could be found easily. The next day, a former 138 Squadron flight commander recalls, the crew that dropped the pigeons would make for the operations room to enquire whether any of the birds had returned. A pigeon dropped in Normandy, for example, could be back in England within hours with its information, scribbled on a scrap of rice paper (supplied in the container) and attached to its leg. The birds' containers also had a two-day supply of food and water, in case they were not found immediately.[27]

Most of the sorties flown by 138 Squadron during 1942 were to France and the Low Countries. Crews disliked the trip to Holland, which was infested with flak, especially along the line of the Friesian Islands, an area where the RAF carried out frequent minelaying operations. The flight across the North Sea was made at zero feet, all the way from the Norfolk coast, the inbound aircraft leapfrogging the dyke that had been built across the mouth of the Zuider Zee and then thundering across that great expanse of water towards its inland objective. On summer nights the route had to be changed because of the distance involved; on these occasions the aircraft had to make the shorter but far more dangerous trip across the 'neck' of Holland between Hoorn and Bergen-tan-Zee, and there were numerous flak batteries along the route. The only chance of survival was to stay as low as possible and run the gauntlet of the fierce 20-mm shell barrage, taking the risk of colliding with one of the many tall church spires that were a prominent feature of the otherwise flat Dutch landscape. Belgium was also heavily defended, but low-flying aircraft were usually able to avoid the worst of the flak here by routing through France. There were quite a few 'quiet spots' on the French coast where an aircraft could slip through, and pilots sometimes chose to penetrate enemy territory as far south as the Cherbourg Peninsula and then route to the east of Paris, well away from the flak zones, on their way up into Belgium.

The very long hauls — to Poland and Czechoslovakia — were infrequent during 1942. The longest trip of all, flown only once, was to a dropping zone south of Bratislava, near the junction of the Czechoslovakian, Hungarian and Austrian borders. On this occasion — which was in the late summer of 1942 — there could be no question of returning home via the same route because there was simply not enough darkness, so the Halifax flew on to Malta. The 1,600 mile flight lasted ten hours, and because of enemy air activity over Malta there was little rest for the crew before they took off again on the return journey, which was made via Gibraltar.

No. 138 Squadron's Operations Record mentions the loss of nine aircraft — three Whitleys and six Halifaxes — during operations in 1942. The heaviest loss was on the night of 20/21 April, when two aircraft, a Whitley and a Halifax, failed to return. The captain of the Halifax was Wing Commander Wally Farley, DFC, the Squadron Commander. The year also saw the loss of the Squadron's first Polish crews, the first of which went missing on an operation to Austria on the night of 19/20 April, in a Halifax. For several months, General Sikorski had been pressing for the establishment of an independent Polish Flight within 138 Squadron to carry out long-range operations to Poland, and also for the provision of more adequate equipment in the shape of aircraft with longer ranges and higher speeds than the Whitley and Halifax. To fulfil the latter requirement he looked to the United States, and in particular to two aircraft types, the Consolidated B-24 Liberator and the Boeing B-17 Flying Fortress.

Both types were already serving with the RAF in limited numbers. Twenty Boeing Fortress Is had entered service with No. 90 Squadron, Bomber Command, early in 1941, but after a year of high-altitude operations over Germany and Norway they had been declared unsuitable due to technical problems (mainly engine and airframe icing at altitude) and withdrawn from first-line service. The greatly improved B-17E Fortress IIA, however, was a much better proposition, and forty-five examples of this new model were delivered to the RAF for service with Coastal Command during 1942. Heavily armed with ten (later thirteen) machine-guns, the Fortress II had a top speed of 300 miles per hour at 30,000 feet and a maximum range of 1,850 miles.

The B-24 Liberator, of which a dozen or so were in service with BOAC on the airline's transatlantic ferry service in 1942, had a performance that was even more favourable to long-range special duties operations. Like the Fortress, it carried a defensive armament of ten machine-guns, but its range was over 2,000 miles, which was the really important factor.

In April 1941, when the United States was still neutral, General Sikorski had sent his Polish Chief of Staff, General Klimecki, to Washington with a secret brief to take up the matter of the supply of a number of long-range aircraft for special duties operations; the proposal was received favourably by the Americans and was discussed further when Sikorski visited the United States at a later date for talks with President Roosevelt. However, these direct negotiations between the representative of the Polish Government in Exile and the Americans did nothing to further Sikorski's cause, for the British Government took an unkindly view of the Poles negotiating such matters independently, and as a result the whole affair became extremely protracted. In fact, negotiations lasted for nearly eighteen months, and it was not until the end of 1942 that agreement for the supply of twelve Liberator bombers for the Polish Air Force in Britain was reached. Even then, the British stipulated that the aircraft would have to be charged to the British Lease-Lend account, which meant that the final approval for their allocation to Polish-manned units would have to be made by the Air Ministry. This did not necessarily mean that they would be used on special operations; they might just as easily be allocated to one of the four Polish bomber squadrons (Nos. 300, 301, 304 and 305) which in 1942 were operating within No. 1 Group, RAF Bomber Command.

In the event, the Secretary of State for Air, Sir Archibald Sinclair, promised Sikorski in January 1943 that three Liberators would be allocated for special duties after they had been adapted for night operations. The remainder would go to Coastal Command. At about the same time the Air Ministry relented and authorized the establishment of a Polish Flight within No. 138 Squadron, bringing the unit up to three-flight status. The Polish Flight was to be equipped with three Halifaxes and three Liberators and was to have six crews, with a seventh in reserve.

Even then, it was to be the summer of 1943 before the Polish Flight received its first Liberators, and in the meantime it was the sturdy and reliable Handley-Page Halifax that bore the brunt of 138 Squadron's operations during that year, the ageing Whitleys having at last been phased out at the end of 1942. And it was while flying Halifaxes that the crews of 138 were to suffer some of their most grievous losses.

4

Maximum Effort: No. 161 Squadron Operations, 1943

Mainly because of adverse weather, operations in 1943 by 161 Squadron got off to a poor start. At St Eval, the Havocs and Albemarles stayed on the ground for most of January, the former because their operations were cancelled and the latter because of unserviceability. Of sixteen Halifax operations flown during January, the first on the night of 14/15, only three were completely successful; five were partly successful, five were not completed, two were abandoned and one aircraft failed to return. The missing Halifax (DG285 'X', captain Pilot Officer Readhead) had set out from Tempsford on the night of 15/16 January with a load of four containers, one parcel and twenty pigeons; its burnt-out remains, with seven bodies on board, were found four miles south of Rennes. It was never established whether the aircraft had been shot down by flak or night-fighters, but the time of the crash was logged as 22.30.[28]

Three Lysander pickup sorties were flown on the night 14/15 January. Squadron Leader Hugh Verity, carrying out his second operation of this kind, landed in a field to the east of Lyons, collected three passengers and returned safely, while John Bridger also picked up three from Thalamy, near Clermont-Ferrand, having made a dangerous and bumpy landing on a field that was covered by a thick growth of heather. Peter Vaughan-Fowler also set out to collect some passengers from a spot near Mâcon, but had to abandon his operation because of heavy cloud.

Two more Lysander sorties were flown on the night of 23/24 January, by Pilot Officers McCairns and F.E. Rymills, DFM. McCairns cruised around his target, a disused airfield at Périgueux, but saw no visual signals and flew home. In fact, a party of German troops had been waiting for him to land; fortunately, the agent McCairns had come to collect — the famous Peter Churchill — had seen the enemy in time and lain low until the danger was past. The other pilot, Rymills, also abandoned his operation, having seen no recognition signal from his target field near Issoudun.

The last Lysander missions in January were carried out on the night of the 26/27. The squadron commander, Wing Commander Pickard, set out for Issoudun with agent Pierre Brossolette as his passenger; arriving in the target area at 01.30, he failed to see any lights, but stayed in the vicinity until 03.15, when he finally spotted the appropriate signal. He landed all right, dropped off Brossolette and picked up two more passengers, Major André Manuel and René Massigli, who had been the French ambassador to Turkey before the war. These were the men, in fact, who should have been collected by Vaughan-Fowler a fortnight earlier. Pickard just managed to scrape in over the English coast, landing at Predannock, in Cornwall, at 06.30 with dry fuel tanks.

On that same night, McCairns and Rymills carried out a double Lysander operation to a field four miles south-west of Lons-le-Saunier, and Hugh Verity, suspecting that more than six passengers might have to be picked up, took along a third aircraft as reserve. On the way, McCairns picked up a recall message and abandoned the operation, returning to base; neither of the other two pilots received the signal and carried on to land at their objective. In the event, only two passengers were awaiting collection, and these were picked up by Rymills.

The bad weather persisted throughout February, and very few operations were flown during this month. On the 13th, the Halifaxes of 'B' Flight were detached to Kinloss, in Scotland, to stand by for an air drop over Norway. Unfortunately, the operation required ideal weather conditions, which did not materialize, and after sitting on the ground for a fortnight the Halifaxes returned to Tempsford. This operation, in fact, had been meant to support a party of Norwegian saboteurs, dropped earlier by 138 Squadron with instructions to attack and destroy the heavy-water plant at Rjukan, which was producing deuterium oxide in connexion with the German atomic bomb project.[29]

On the night of 13/14 February, the former King's Flight Lockheed Hudson N7263 'O' for Orange, which had spent much of its time sitting in a hangar at Tempsford, finally got its chance to take part in operations. For some time, Wing Commander Pickard had been experimenting with this aircraft, endeavouring to find out in how short a distance he could land it; by knocking twenty knots off the recommended approach speed, coming 'over the fence' at just over 55 knots, cutting the engines just before the wheels touched and then applying full brake as soon as the tail settled, he discovered that he could bring the twin-engined machine to a standstill in 350 yards.

To achieve this in practice, on a familiar airfield, was one thing; to land a Hudson in a hastily-prepared field in enemy territory, under operational conditions, was quite another. But on the night of the 13/14 February Pickard, full of confidence, flew to a field at St Yan, near Roanne, and landed the Hudson safely with five agents on board, bringing back mail on the return flight. The trip was completely uneventful, which could not be said of some Hudson operations that would be carried out by 161 in the future. On this first occasion, Pickard's navigator was Pilot Officer Taylor, a Canadian, and his wireless operator/air gunner was Sergeant Henry Figg, who had been with N7263 since its King's Flight days.

A double Lysander operation was also flown on the night of 13/14 February, when Vaughan-Fowler and McCairns flew to Lons-le-Saunier, landing three passengers and picking up four between them. Hugh Verity went along as spare, but he was not required; the operation was completely trouble-free. Flying Officer Rymills also made a pickup on the night of 19/20 February, landing one agent at Feurs, west of Lyon, and bringing out two more.

The Hudson, with the same crew as before, made its second trip into France on the following night, landing near Arles to disembark one passenger and pick up six. This sortie was also completed without difficulty, but it was a different story on the night of 24/25 February, when Pickard, Taylor and Figg, together with Flight Lieutenant Putt of 138 Squadron, took N7263 into a field near Dijon, between Tournus and Cuisery. Pickard had his right hand and wrist in plaster, having fallen off a beam in the bar of the Mess at Tempsford during a prank a few days earlier, so Figg worked the throttles for him and operated the flaps and undercarriage. After making a number of circuits of his target while waiting for the flarepath to be lit, he eventually landed a little to one side of the lights, and when he tried to turn the aircraft at the end of its landing run it became bogged down in a patch of soft ground.

Fortunately, a lot of people were present on the landing ground, and after a great deal of pushing the Hudson came free, enabling Pickard to taxi towards the light at which he was to begin his take-off run, but after a few hundred yards the main wheels sank into the mud again. No amount of pushing would free it this time, so the reception committee brought a team of horses from a nearby farm and harnessed them to the aircraft's main oleos. With their help, the Hudson was finally pulled clear, and the pilot turned its nose in what he hoped was the right direction for take-off. He managed to get airborne all right, but some tree branches at the far end of the field neatly removed two feet of the aircraft's starboard wingtip. However, the sturdy Hudson remained in the air and Pickard set course for the French coast at 05.30, two hours after he had touched down. The Hudson crossed the coast near le Havre at 07.03, just as dawn was breaking, and Pickard — mindful of the danger from patrolling enemy fighters — radioed Tangmere to arrange an escort of Hawker Typhoons. This duly arrived as the Hudson flew across the Channel, and the aircraft made a safe landing. There is some doubt about the number of passengers carried on this trip, although Peter Churchill, who was present at the landing ground, recorded later that he had seen ten men disembark and ten more board the aircraft.[30]

Two more Lysander sorties were flown before the end of the month, both of them by Squadron Leader Verity and both of them abortive. On the first trip, flown on the night of 24/25 February, Verity found the target area near Châteauroux blanketed by fog and returned to base, which to his dismay was also fogbound. He groped his way down through the murk with the aid of searchlights, but flared out too high and dropped his aircraft like a stone thirty feet on to the ground, smashing its undercarriage and piling it up on its nose. Fortunately, neither the pilot nor his passenger sustained any injury. Verity made a second attempt on the following night. On this occasion there was no fog and he found the target, but when he looked for the visual signal he saw a series of rapid dots — the danger sign — being flashed at him from the ground. He quickly turned away and headed for home.

March 1943, was a tragic month for 161 Squadron's Halifax Flight, with two aircraft missing on operations and one destroyed in a crash landing. The first Halifax to be lost was DG245 'W' (Flight Lieutenant Prior) which failed to return from operations on the night of 14/15 March; the second was DG244 'Y' (Flying Officer Wynn), which went missing on the night of 18/19 March. The third aircraft, DG283, crash-landed at Henley-on-Thames as a result of engine failure; two of the seven-man crew were killed. Because of these losses, very few Halifax operations were flown during the March moon period.

Following continual unserviceability, the Albemarle detachment at St Eval was finally disbanded during March and the personnel returned to Tempsford, although the Havoc detachment remained at St Eval to carry out special radio trials (of which more later).

For the Lysander Flight, March was a month of successes. The first (double) Lysander operation was flown on the night of 17/18 March, when Flying Officers Rymills and Vaughan-Fowler flew to a location near Poitiers carrying four agents between them. Vaughan-Fowler had a nasty moment when, following a bumpy landing, long flames belched from his engine exhaust; acting quickly, he at once turned off the petrol and ignition, jumped from the cockpit and smothered the fire with his Mae West lifejacket. With the flames out, he calmly re-started the engine and taxied across the field to where the reception committee was waiting. Both he and Rymills, who had landed twenty minutes earlier, picked up their agents and returned safely to Tangmere.

There were three single Lysander sorties on the night of 19/20 March, of which two were successful. The one that failed was flown by Flying Officer Rymills, who set out for a field near Villefranche but did not find it and returned to base. The others were flown by Squadron Leader Verity, who went to Arras to disembark three agents and collect three more, and John Bridger, who landed in a field near St Yan to disembark agents Jean Moulin, General Delestraint and Christian Pineau. The

Lysander had hardly taken off, and the agents got clear of the landing ground, when the Germans arrived.

The next night, Wing Commander Pickard flew to Villefranche with one agent in his Lysander and successfully picked up three more; Pierre Dallas, Dr Zimmern and Colonel Delamaire, the men who ought to have been collected twenty-four hours earlier by Rymills. Pickard experienced no problems on this sortie. Neither did Hugh Verity, who flew the last Lysander trip of the month on the night of the 23/24, landing two agents at Compiegne and bringing out two more, one of whom was Peter Churchill.

Thanks mainly to the excellent weather conditions that prevailed during the moon period, April 1943 broke all records for successful sorties by 161 Squadron. The Halifaxes carried out 57 individual sorties, of which 32 were completely successful and many of the others partially so.[31]

The pickup Flight's operations for the month were kicked off on the night of 13/14 April with a double Lysander trip to a landing ground between Mâcon and Manziat; this was flown by Squadron Leader Verity and Flying Officer Rymills and was completely uneventful, the pilots disembarking two agents and bringing out four.

The next night, Flying Officers Vaughan-Fowler and McCairns flew another double Lysander sortie, this time to a strip two miles north-east of Amboise, to disembark four agents and collect one. It was a cloudy night, with little moonlight over the target area, and McCairns, who was making a low, slow approach to land, smashed through the branches of a tree just before touchdown. The man in charge of the reception committee told him that only the aerial appeared to have been torn away and that there was no sign of any other damage, but when McCairns got airborne again he soon discovered that something was seriously wrong. The whole aircraft was vibrating badly, and the oil temperature was in the red sector of the gauge.

McCairns climbed steadily through the cloud, with the aircraft still trembling under his hands, but after a few minutes the engine spluttered and died. The pilot trimmed the aircraft to glide, warned his passenger to be ready for a forced landing, and tried to sort out what was wrong. At 3,000 feet he suddenly

English Channel

CHERBOURG
LE HAVRE   ROUEN   ST-SA
OUISTREHAM
TROUVILLE
BAYEUX   CABOURG   PERRIERS
CAEN   FLEUR
LES ANDE

FALAISE

CHANNEL
ISLANDS

DREU

ALENCON   CHARTR

NOGENT-
LE-ROTROU

LE MANS

VENDON

CHARTRE   BLC
ANGERS   Loir
NANTES   TOURS   AMB
LOIRE   SAUMUR   CHENONCE
AZAY-LE-RIDEAU
VA

CHATTELLERAULT

POITIERS

LA CHA

Atlantic Ocean

Charente   ANGOULEME

MONTIGNAC

PERIGU

BORDEAUX

PRINCIPAL PICK-UP POINT

FRANCE (161 SQUADRON)

R.McM. 82

found the trouble; the carburettor hot air control had slipped out of place, with the result that the carburettor had frozen up. He quickly rectified this, and after another few hundred feet the engine burst into life again. When he inspected the damage after landing at Tangmere, McCairns realized how lucky he had been. The Lysander's tailplane had almost been ripped loose and was held on by a solitary screw, the big auxiliary fuel tank had a hole in it, the exhaust was choked with bits of wood and the propeller spinner was crushed. As a result of this incident, the order went out for all 161 Squadron pilots to switch on their landing lights before touchdown on an unfamiliar field.

There were four operations on the night of 15/16 April: three Lysander — one a double — and one Hudson. The latter was flown by Wing Commander Pickard, with Flying Officer Alan Broadley as his navigator and Flying Officer Cocker as wireless operator. Broadley, who came from the lovely little market town of Richmond, in north Yorkshire, had crewed with Pickard since 1940; the two were to remain together until that tragic and heroic day in February 1944 when, flying a Mosquito, they were to lose their lives in the famous attack on the walls of Amiens Prison.

On this Hudson mission, Pickard, in addition to two agents and a load of baggage, carried a pair of unauthorized passengers: Wing Commanders Brooks and Lockhart, who had gone along for the ride. Their presence on board the aircraft should have presented no problems, because Pickard expected to pick up only four passengers for the return trip, but when he landed at Pont-de-Vaux he found no fewer than eleven people waiting. Since the maximum number of passengers a Hudson could safely carry was ten, Pickard regretfully had to turn away three of the waiting Frenchmen.

The single Lysander trips involved a flight to Lyons by John Bridger, delivering four packages and picking up three agents, and one to a field north of Tours by Hugh Verity, disembarking two agents and picking up one. On this sortie, Verity's Lysander sustained damage to its tailwheel on landing.

The double Lysander sortie was flown by Flying Officers Vaughan-Fowler and McCairns, who landed fourteen miles north-east of Les Andelys, in the Rouen area, to disembark three agents and bring back five between them. One of the passengers

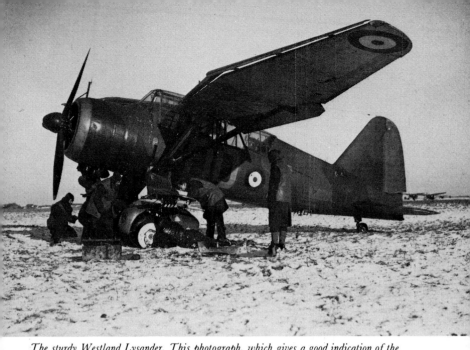

The sturdy Westland Lysander. This photograph, which gives a good indication of the aircraft's size, depicts a Mk. II of No. 13 Squadron in France, February 1940. The serial number has been painted out and there are bomb racks under the rear fuselage as well as on stub wings.

A Lysander kicks up powdery snow as it taxies out for take-off.

Lysanders modified for special operations were known by the works title Lysander SCW (Special Contract Westland). These photographs show two Mk. IIIAs, V9287 and V9738, the former (above) retaining a normal camouflage scheme and the latter finished black overall. The black paintwork was later dropped as it showed up the aircraft in silhouette against a cloud background. (Westland Aircraft Limited)

on the homeward run was Wing Commander F.F.E. Yeo-Thomas, the famous 'White Rabbit', whose SOE exploits were later to become legendary.[32]

There were three single Lysander sorties on the night of 16/17 April, and on one of these Flight Lieutenant John Bridger had a very close shave indeed. Approaching his designated field near Clermont-Ferrand, he touched down too fast and too far past the first light, so he opened the throttle to go round again — and flew straight into a high-tension cable stretched across the far end of the field. The darkness dissolved in a vivid blue-white flash, but although he was temporarily blinded Bridger managed to keep the aircraft flying. Circling round the field, he made another approach and this time brought the aircraft in for what should have been a perfect landing. What he did not know, however, was that one of his tyres had burst when he hit the cable and the machine swung wildly before he manged to bring it to a stop.

Bridger unloaded two packages, told the two agents he had come to collect to board the aircraft, and then wondered what to do. With a burst tyre it would be almost impossible to get the Lysander out of the field, which was uneven. After a few moments' thought he did the only thing possible; he took out his .38 Service revolver and put a bullet through the Lysander's good tyre. It took several bullets before the tyre slowly deflated, and with the aircraft's equilibrium restored — albeit somewhat shakily — Bridger decided to attempt the take-off. Fortunately, the ground was hard and the Lysander rose into the air well clear of the far boundary. It arrived back at Tangmere with several yards of copper wire trailing behind it.

Of the other two Lysander sorties that night, one — flown by Pickard — was abandoned when no visual signals were received from the designated field near Montrichard, while the second, carried out by Flying Officer Rymills, was a complete success, the pilot landing three agents near Villefranche and taking out three more. On the night of the 18/19 Pickard carried out another Hudson sortie, flying a load of freight into a well-selected field near Florac and bringing out eight passengers, and the following night McCairns flew to Montrichard, which had been Pickard's destination on the 16/17. This time the flarepath was lit and the recognition signal flashed, so McCairns went ahead and touched down. It was a bumpy landing and his engine cut out, but he restarted it and taxied round to where four passengers were waiting for him. He took off with difficulty, for the Lysander was badly overloaded, and set a homeward course in poor weather. At one point his engine stopped again, but he quickly changed fuel tanks and that cured the trouble. He reached Tangmere safely after evading some flak over the French coast near Cap de la Hague.

The last week of the moon period saw two double Lysander operations, the first on the night of 20/21 April when 'Bunny' Rymills and Peter Vaughan-Fowler flew to Montignac near Angoulême, landing four agents and safely bringing out four more. On 22/23 April it was the turn of Hugh Verity and John Bridger; Verity went in first and found only one passenger waiting on the strip near Le Mans, so Bridger was ordered not to land.

On 6 May 1943 No. 161 Squadron received a new commanding officer. Pickard was promoted to Group Captain and posted to command RAF Station Lissett, in East Yorkshire; his replacement was Wing Commander L. Mc D. Hodges, who had been 'B' Flight Commander.

The Squadron suffered no operational losses during May, but a tragic accident on the 16th took the life of one of 161's new pilots, Pilot Officer Jack Bartrum. His Lysander stalled on the approach to land during a training flight, crashed and burst into flames.

The Halifaxes flew twenty-three sorties during the month, and the Havoc detachment at St Eval sixteen, most of them unsuccessful. These aircraft were engaged in a radio trials project known as 'Ascension', which involved the relaying of radio messages from agents on the Continent to air and ground stations. During this period, No. 161 also had two Lockheed Ventura aircraft temporarily on its inventory. On 28 May, they were turned over to a new unit that formed at Tempsford, along with three Halifaxes; this was No. 1575 Flight, which eventually became No. 624 Squadron, earmarked for special duties operations in the Mediterranean.

Two Lysander sorties, one a double, were carried out on the night of 13/14 May. Flying Officer McCairns flew the single, landing one agent and collecting three from a field near

Montrichard, while the double was flown by Squadron Leader Verity and Flying Officer Rymills. They landed at Azay-sur-Cher, near Tours, unloading four agents (together with fourteen large suitcases and packages) and bringing out one. The latter was Major Francis Suttill, known by the code-name 'Prosper', who controlled one of the biggest Underground groups in France.

The first Hudson sortie of the month was a failure. The aircraft, piloted by the station commander, Group Captain E.H. Fielden, set out for the Plaine de Chanet on the night of 15/16 May, but was unable to land because of fog in the target area. The same pilot, with Squadron Leader Wagland as his navigator and Flying Officer Cocker as wireless operator, was successful on his second attempt on the night of the 19/20, unloading three agents and taking aboard six, one of whom was the French General Georges (who had commanded the Northern Army Group at the time of the Blitzkrieg in May 1940). The Hudson did not make its landing until 02.15, and Fielden, reluctant to take the risk of being caught in daylight by enemy fighters during the return trip over northern France, decided to divert to North Africa. The Hudson landed safely at Maison Blanche, near Algiers, and Fielden flew back to England via Gibraltar later that day.

A second Hudson sortie that night was flown by Squadron Leader Verity, with Flight Lieutenant Livry and Sergeant Shine as his crew. The aircraft was the second Hudson allocated to 161 Squadron, N7221, and it was Verity's first operational Hudson pickup. All went smoothly, the Hudson depositing one agent and twenty-four packages in a field near Lons-le-Saunier and bringing eight agents home.

A Lysander sortie by John Bridger on the night of 20/21 May had to be abandoned because of fog in the target area, but on a second attempt the next night he landed successfully near Issoudun, dropping off five packages and bringing out two agents. There was another Lysander sortie that night, flown by Peter Vaughan-Fowler to Compiegne, but no recognition signals were seen and the operation was abandoned. Vaughan-Fowler's passenger on this occasion was the agent Noor Inayat Khan, who was later to become one of the heroines — and martyrs — of the Resistance.

June 1943 was a generally successful month, although marred by the loss of two Halifaxes on operations. These were DG406 (Flight Lieutenant Foster) and DG405 (Pilot Officer Higgins). The former aircraft also carried Squadron Leader Walker, who had just been appointed to command the Halifax Flight. One of these aircraft (DG405) apparently came down in the sea, because the bodies of two crew members (Sergeants Hartin and Watson) were later washed ashore. The loss of two complete crews was the main contributory factor to the relatively few Halifax operations carried out during the moon period by 161 Squadron.

At St Eval, the Havoc detachment enjoyed some unaccustomed success, establishing several good contacts on their airborne 'Ascension' sorties. The Lysanders were detached to Tangmere as usual during the moon period and the month started with two 'doubles', the first on 11/12 June when Vaughan-Fowler and McCairns flew to the Tours area. This operation was abandoned because no signals were seen, but the same two pilots went back again the following night and this time were successful, disembarking five passengers and picking up six. Vaughan-Fowler and McCairns were airborne once more on 15/16 June, flying to Estrées St Denis, where they unloaded and picked up an unrecorded number of passengers. In a second Lysander operation that night, Flying Officer Rymills landed two passengers and picked up three more at a strip near Bouillancy, north-east of Paris.

There was also a Hudson sortie on the night of 15/16 June; this was flown by Squadron Leader Verity, with his usual crew of Flight Lieutenant Livry and Sergeant Shine. The aircraft was N7221, and Verity carried two passengers and fourteen packages to a field near Mâcon, where he landed in pitch darkness and driving rain. Taking off again with eight passengers on board, Verity decided — as Fielden had done on a previous trip — that there was a risk of being caught over enemy territory in daylight if he headed straight back to England, so he turned south-west and headed across the Mediterranean to Algiers, landing at Maison Blanche at 06.50. He resumed the flight as soon as the Hudson had been refuelled and his passengers and crew had breakfasted, returning home that same day via Gibraltar.

76

There were two Lysander operations on the night of 16/17 June, one a single by Peter Vaughan-Fowler, who flew to Châteauroux to pick up two agents, and the other a double by McCairns and Rymills, who landed four passengers near Angers and brought out five. Rymills had a further success on 20/21, bringing a lone agent from a field north of Blois, and Verity also set out on this night for a strip three miles north-west of Amboise, but failed to see any visual signals and flew home. A second attempt on the night of 22/23 June had to be abandoned when Verity's Lysander suffered generator failure over the English coast, with the loss of all electrical services, but he completed the mission on the following night, disembarking two passengers and flying out two others. Verity records that on this occasion he attempted the landing before the moon had risen, in pitch darkness, and frightened himself so badly on the approach that he made up his mind never to try a similar thing again.

July brought a spell of bad weather during the all-important moon period, but despite this No. 161 Squadron achieved excellent results. The Halifaxes undertook 28 sorties, of which 24 were completed successfully for the loss of one aircraft, piloted by Sergeant Crome, on the night of 22/23 July. During this month more crews — including one composed entirely of Norwegians — were posted to the Halifax Flight from No. 24 Operational Training Unit to replace tour-expired personnel.

Squadron Leader Verity carried out the first Lysander operation of the month, on the night of the 14/15, picking up one passenger from a strip south of Bourges. With him on this trip he took Flight Lieutenant Stephen Hankey, a newcomer to the Squadron, so that the new pilot could gain operational experience. There were three Lysander operations on the night of 15/16 July, one of them a double which was flown by McCairns and Vaughan-Fowler to a field west of Tours, where they landed two agents and picked up four. The single sorties were flown by Squadron Leader Verity, who collected a passenger from a location north of Orleans, and Flying Officer Rymills, who picked up two agents from a strip south-west of Auxerre. It was 'Bunny' Rymills' last pickup operation, for he was posted away from Tempsford shortly afterwards. He survived the war and, after a successful spell in farming, founded his own electronics engineering firm in Cambridge.

The Squadron now had a third Hudson on its inventory, T9465, and on 16/17 July Group Captain Fielden flew this aircraft to a spot east of Lyons with two agents on board. Unfortunately he saw no recognition signals in the target area, so he flew on across the Mediterranean and landed at Maison Blanche. While the crew and passengers were having a meal, a Blenheim bomber with engine trouble skidded off the runway on landing and ploughed into the parked Hudson, severely damaging the latter's port wing. Crew and passengers returned to England in a Lancaster, via Gibraltar.

Two pickup operations were carried out on 17/18 July, both by Lysanders. One was a failure, because the pilot, McCairns, saw no visual signals and had to come home with his two passengers still on board, but the other was a complete success. Peter Vaughan-Fowler, newly promoted to Flight Lieutenant, deposited three agents on a disused airstrip at Betz-Bouillancy, north of Paris, and flew three more home. McCairns succeeded in completing his mission two nights later, landing two agents and embarking three at Azay-sur-Cher, near Tours.

A double Lysander trip to Châteauroux was made by Hugh Verity and Peter Vaughan-Fowler on 21/22 July, the two pilots taking out three passengers and bringing back seven, the latter including the wife of Jacques Robert, a leading agent, and their two small daughters. Verity recounts the charming story of how the little girls, on asking how they were to reach England, were told that they would be spirited there by the Holy Ghost. More than thirty years later, Verity — who had written about the incident in a Sunday newspaper — received a letter that began 'Dear Holy Ghost'. It was from one of those small girls, now grown up and married, who recalled the flight vividly, and the joy of arriving in the free atmosphere of England.[33]

On 22/23 July the new Squadron Commander, Wing Commander Hodges, made his first operational trip with 161, flying three passengers to Angers and collecting three more, all of them Belgians. The other sortie that night — a single Lysander to Soissons, flown by McCairns — had to be abandoned because of thick, low cloud that covered the entire route.

On 24/25 July, Hugh Verity, accompanied by Squadron Leader Livry and Sergeant Shine, set out in a Hudson for Lyons, carrying the two much-travelled agents who had attempted to reach the same destination with Group Captain Fielden a few nights earlier. This time the landing ground was located and Verity, after disembarking his passengers, took on eight more. The take-off was tricky, because the Hudson's port engine suffered a momentary loss of power, and the aircraft's undercarriage ripped through the boundary hedge, but no serious damage was caused and Verity flew on to Maison Blanche, returning to England by the usual route on 27 July.

The last sortie of the month was again flown by McCairns, and again it ended in failure because of low cloud and extremely poor visibility. In searching for his objective, McCairns flew directly over an airfield, which he thought to be Creil, and the defences opened up with every conceivable kind of anti-aircraft weapon. He was very lucky to get away.

Operations for the month of August were highly successful and broke all previous records. The Halifax Flight was now in a much better position, having nine crews on strength and a Halifax in reserve. The Flight carried out fifty-five successful sorties during the moon period. The Havoc detachment at St Eval also enjoyed better fortune, making continuous contact on every sortie with operators in France and Belgium.

Out of twelve Lysander sorties flown in August there was only one failure, and that was on the first night of the moon period, 14/15 August, when bad weather prevented Flight Lieutenant Robin Hooper from locating his target field near Dreux. On that same night, however, Vaughan-Fowler and McCairns made a successful double Lysander trip to Bourges, delivering three passengers and bringing out five. Hooper found his field all right on the following night, disembarking one passenger and taking two on board. He was forced to hurry his take-off when car headlights were seen approaching the field, but he got airborne without trouble and flew safely back to Tangmere. It was his first Lysander pickup. There were two more Lysander operations that night, one of them a double flown by Squadron Leader Verity and Flying Officer McCairns. They landed four passengers and picked up five at Couture-sur-Loire, north of Tours. The single trip was made by Peter Vaughan-Fowler, who dropped off two agents at the old airfield of Betz-Bouillancy, north-east of Paris, and collected three.

Verity was airborne again on the following night (16/17 August), flying a package to Couture and bringing out three passengers. En route to the target, he had the depressing experience of seeing an aircraft shot down in flames only a couple of miles ahead of him, presumably by a night-fighter. Apart from that, the flight was uneventful.

The night of the 19/20 saw August's first Hudson pickup. This was made by Wing Commander Hodges, who flew to a strip near the Loire to land one passenger and pick up ten. The landing was difficult, for there was a lot of ground mist that diffused the beams of the reception committee's torches and made it hard to judge their exact position. It was as well that the mist prevented Hodges from seeing another obstacle: a herd of terrified bullocks, which stampeded across the strip just before he touched down. The other operation that night was a single Lysander, flown by Vaughan-Fowler to a strip north of Villefranche. The trip was uneventful, the pilot landing one passenger and collecting two.

The next night's Lysander operations consisted of two 'doubles', both of them completely without incident. One was flown by McCairns and Hooper, who landed two passengers near Chartres and brought out four, and the other by Verity and Vaughan-Fowler, who also brought home four agents after landing one at a strip near Toury, north of Orleans.

The moon period was rounded off by two Hudson sorties, one flown on the night of 22/23 August and the other on the following night. The first trip was made by Squadron Leader Verity and failed because dense fog prevented a landing in the target area near Mâcon; Wing Commander Hodges completed the operation twenty-four hours later, landing one passenger and bringing out eight.

Despite the fact that bad weather prevailed at the start of the September moon period, which made it impossible to carry out operations, a very good performance was put up by 161 Squadron over the period as a whole. 'B' Flight (Halifaxes) was now in a very strong position with regard to personnel, its nine operational crews having been joined by a tenth which was undergoing training. The Halifaxes carried out thirty-seven sorties with very few failures, and most of these were due to no reception lights being seen in the target areas. Towards the end of the moon period, three Short Stirling bombers, together with their crews, were attached to Tempsford from No. 214 Squadron, which was based at Chedburgh in Suffolk. The purpose was to assess the Stirling's suitability for dropping agents and supplies, but conditions were none too favourable and only six sorties were flown by the new arrivals before the end of the moon period. It was decided to retain the Stirlings for further trials during the October period.[34]

At St Eval, the Havocs made twelve sorties, of which eight were successful. Three Hudsons were now standing by to take over the Havocs' radio trials role, but these aircraft were not yet operational because they were still undergoing modifications.

The Lysander Flight had an exceptionally busy September period, starting on the night of the 10/11 when two sorties were flown, one of them a double. The pilots, Hooper and McCairns, ran into bad weather en route and called off the operation. Peter Vaughan-Fowler flew a successful single, picking up three passengers from a strip near Reims. Hooper and McCairns completed their operation the next night, delivering six passengers to a location near Bourges and bringing out another six.

On the following night, 12/13 September, 161 Squadron carried out the first 'treble' Lysander operation. Three aircraft, flown by Squadron Leader Verity, Flight Lieutenant Vaughan-Fowler and Flying Officer McCairns, flew to a field half a mile north-east of Rivarennes, in Touraine. The operation went without a hitch, and the time between the first Lysander touching down to the last one taking off was exactly nine minutes. The three aircraft landed eight passengers between them and took out a further eight.

Three Lysander sorties were undertaken on the night of 13/14 September, but one of them — flown by Robin Hooper — was abortive, the pilot failing to sight any reception lights at his destination. Hugh Verity successfully collected three passengers, including two RAF aircrew who had managed to evade capture after being shot down, from the Reims area after circling for more than an hour; when he finally saw the recognition signal and landed, he had his work cut out to avoid some haystacks which were uncomfortably close to the flarepath. The other Lysander pilot who was airborne that night, Flight Lieutenant Stephen Hankey, collected one passenger from Dreux and made it safely back to Tangmere, despite a total electrical failure on the way home.

Hankey had less luck on the following night, when he carried out a double Lysander operation to Cottainville, north of Orleans, together with another newcomer to 161 Squadron, Flying Officer J.R.G. Bathgate. The latter pilot found the target field and landed to collect three passengers, but Hankey failed to spot the lights and flew home with an empty aircraft. The other trip that night was made by Wing Commander Hodges in a Hudson, which he flew to a strip near Lons-le-Saunier with eight agents on board. He took on four passengers and waited ten minutes for more to turn up, but when they failed to arrive he decided to take off and head for home.

There was only one Lysander trip on 15/16 September, when Robin Hooper successfully collected two passengers from Betz-Bouillancy, near Compiegne, after landing three others. Two operations, one a double, were flown on the following night; the old team of McCairns and Vaughan-Fowler flew to Compiegne and exchanged one passenger for six, while the single Lysander sortie, flown by Hankey, was called off when no reception was seen. There was another double on the night of 17/18 September, carried out by Hodges and Bathgate, who landed four agents at a strip near Angers and brought out six, and on that same night Hugh Verity took a load of packages to Rouen and brought home four evading Allied aircrew.

Stephen Hankey enjoyed better fortune on the night of 18/19 September, successfully landing one agent near Orleans and bringing out another, together with a load of parcels. Also on that night, McCairns and Vaughan-Fowler flew another of their doubles to a field eight miles north of Angoulême and landed four agents (one of whom was Wing Commander Yeo-Thomas) before taking aboard four more.

A lone mission to Châteauroux on 19/20 September failed because of adverse weather, the pilot — Robin Hooper — failing to locate the target field, but Flying Officer Bathgate found the same field on the next night and brought home four passengers, even though weather conditions were still poor.

The last pickup of the September moon period was made on the night of 21/22, when Squadron Leader Verity, accompanied by Squadron Leader Livry and Sergeant Shine, flew a Hudson to a strip five miles south-east of Tournus (Saone) and landed four passengers, together with a load of packages. It was a difficult trip from the navigational point of view because of low cloud all the way to the target and back again, but Verity touched down safely on his third attempt and brought out eight more passengers.

All operations were severely handicapped by bad weather during October 1943. Nevertheless, the Halifaxes carried out forty-six sorties, although a fair number of operations had to be abandoned when no reception signals were seen. One of the month's best efforts was that of Flying Officer Bell and his Halifax crew, who made a 2,000-mile round trip from Kinloss to Narvik, in Norway, and dropped an agent's equipment right on target in very poor weather. There was one casualty during the month, when a Halifax captained by Flight Sergeant Lewis failed to return on the night of 20/21 October. The three Stirlings from 214 Squadron were joined by another three for operations during the October moon period, but these six aircraft carried out only twenty-one sorties, and of these only a fraction were successful. The additional three Stirlings returned to their parent unit at the end of the period.

Five 'Ascension' sorties were flown by the St Eval Havoc detachment during the month, and one of these had to be hurriedly abandoned when the oxygen supply failed at high altitude. On 29 October, three Hudsons arrived at St Eval to take over the 'Ascension' duties from the Havocs, and on the last day of the month one of the Hudsons took part in a lengthy air-sea rescue operation over the Channel.

The first three pickup attempts — one by a Hudson (Wing Commander Hodges) and two by Lysanders (both Flight Lieutenant Hooper) — failed through bad weather, but on the fourth attempt Flight Lieutenant Hankey landed two agents near Amboise on the night of 16/17 October and brought out three. In a second Lysander operation that night, Flying Officer Bathgate set out for Compiegne, but received faulty radio bearings from the ground station on the south coast of England and arrived over France miles off track. He was unable to fix his position, and flew home. In another Lysander, Jimmy McCairns, heading for the same objective, also had trouble with radio bearings, but after an hour's searching he managed to pinpoint his position and eventually reached his objective, landing two passengers and collecting three.

Also on 16/17 October, Hugh Verity set out in a Hudson to complete the operation which Hodges had called off earlier. With him, as second pilot, went Pilot Officer John Affleck, who had recently transferred to pickup operations from the Halifaxes of 'B' Flight. The sortie was uneventful, Verity making a safe landing near Mâcon to disembark five passengers and collect eight, one of whom was General de Lattre de Tassigny, who was later to take command of the French First Army and who, at the end of the war, would represent France at the surrender of Germany.

There were three Lysander operations on the night of 17/18 October, one of them a double. This was flown by McCairns and Bathgate and went off without a hitch, the pilots exchanging six passengers at a strip near Châteauroux. Hugh Verity also landed one and brought out two from the Rouen area, but the third sortie that night, flown by Stephen Hankey, failed because the pilot was unable to locate the target in thick ground mist.

On the following night, 161 Squadron carried out its first double-Hudson operation, made necessary by the fact that no fewer than eighteen passengers were awaiting collection from Lons-le-Saunier. The two Hudsons were flown by Wing Commander Bob Hodges and Pilot Officer John Affleck, carrying four outward-bound passengers between them. Both pilots found the target field without difficulty and Hodges landed safely on the first attempt, but Affleck misjudged his approach and had to go round again. On the second try he carved through the tops of some poplars and touched down slightly off target, frightening the life out of the agent in charge of the reception committee, Paul Rivière, who threw himself flat just in time; in fact, the Hudson's main wheels touched the ground on either side of him. All eighteen passengers — including Vincent Auriol, who after the war was to become President of France — were flown safely to England, although 161 Squadron's Operations Record Book states bluntly that double Hudson trips were 'not to be recommended'.

There were two Lysander trips that night, although one of

84

them failed because the pilot, McCairns, found no reception at the target field near Compiegne. The other sortie was flown by a newcomer to the Lysander Flight, Flying Officer J. McBride, who successfully landed one passenger at a strip north of Orleans and brought out three.

John Affleck took a Hudson to France again on the night of 20/21 October, exchanging four passengers for another four at a field north of Angers. A double Lysander operation that night, flown by Hooper and Bathgate to Angoulême, failed because of bad visibility in the target area, but on a third sortie Hugh Verity exchanged three agents at a strip north-west of Chartres. The last pickup operation of the month was flown on the following night and was a 'double'; McCairns was one of the pilots, but the name of the other is not on record. Two agents were landed and three collected from Nogent-sur-Seine, east of Paris, the Lysander pilots having to thread their way through some very severe weather, including thunderstorms.

Worsening weather again severely curtailed operations during November, but the 'B' Flight Halifaxes nevertheless managed thirty-four sorties, a high proportion of which failed because of bad visibility or because no reception lights were seen. One Halifax (Pilot Officer Line) failed to return from operations on the night of 10/11 November, and a few days later another, piloted by Flight Lieutenant Gray, was completely written off when it swung off the runway on take-off and collided with a steamroller. Fortunately, only one of the crew was hurt, the rear gunner, Pilot Officer Pearse, who sustained spinal injuries.

The six Stirlings from 214 Squadron once again flew over to Tempsford for operations during the moon period and flew twenty-four sorties, but most of these were failures and the record of these aircraft to date was generally unimpressive. At St Eval, however, the Hudsons got into full stride on their 'Ascension' operations and flew fourteen sorties, in the course of which they established regular contact with SOE operatives across the Channel.

The month's first Lysander sortie was flown by Flying Officer Bathgate on the night of 6/7 November, and three agents were collected from a field south-west of Paris. On the next night, Flying Officer McCairns landed one agent at Compiegne and brought home four passengers — all USAAF aircrew who had been shot down — in a badly overloaded aircraft. A 'double' to Bourges by Squadron Leader Verity and Flying Officer McBride on 8/9 November took out six passengers and brought a similar number home, but a treble Lysander operation to Châtellerault on the following night was frustrated by the weather, which was truly appalling. The pilots on this occasion were Hodges, Hooper and Hankey. Jimmy McCairns also set out for Compiegne that night, but he too was forced to turn back.

Three Lysander operations, one a treble and one a double, were attempted on the night of 11/12 November. The treble, to Châtellerault, was flown by Hooper, Bathgate and McCairns; Robin Hooper landed first and disembarked two agents, but he found the field extremely soft and told the other two pilots not to attempt a landing. Hooper himself experienced considerable difficulty in getting his Lysander out of the mud and taking off. The double operation, to a location west of Reims, was undertaken by Hugh Verity and Stephen Hankey, who picked up six passengers between them, and the third trip of the night was made to Vendôme by Flying Officer McBride. This was a failure, because — as it was later discovered — the reception committee had had a brush with German troops and had consequently not arrived at the field.

Squadron Leader Verity carried out another successful mission on the following night, flying to Compiegne together with Bathgate. The two of them landed four passengers and brought home three.

The night of 15/16 November saw the month's first Hudson pickup, when Wing Commander Hodges, with Squadron Leader Wagland navigating, flew to Angers to land five passengers and pick up ten, including five aircrew. Tragically, some of the agents disembarked by Hodges were captured almost immediately by the Germans, who had watched the whole operation from hiding. There were three Lysander operations that night, of which one — flown by Verity and Hankey to Amboise — failed because of a lack of reception. The night's second 'double', however, carried out by Bathgate and McBride, was a complete success, four passengers being disembarked at Angoulême and eight picked up, including seven Allied aircrew. On the third sortie, Flying Officer McCairns reached his objective in pouring rain — after crossing the Pas de Calais defences at only 500 feet without a shot being fired at him — and landed at Arras, dropping off two passengers and taking on three. One of the latter was the redoubtable Wing Commander Yeo-Thomas.

There were three Lysander operations on the following night, too, but one of them — flown by Stephen Hankey to Vierzon — had to be abandoned when the pilot found cloud extending right down to ground level en route. Verity and McCairns carried out a 'double' to Compiegne, landing two passengers and bringing out six, of whom five were once again shot-down aircrew.

The third sortie that night ended in drama. Robin Hooper, landing at Châtellerault, became hopelessly bogged down, and no amount of pushing would free the Lysander. After several hours, during which the aircraft still stubbornly refused to budge even when bullocks were hitched to it, Hooper decided to give up and set fire to the machine, making his getaway with the reception committee. He was hidden by the French Underground, and eventually returned to England by Lysander in December.

Hooper's Lysander was the first of 161 Squadron's pickup aircraft to be lost on operations, and it seemed now that the run of good luck which the Squadron had enjoyed for fifteen months was to be brutally shattered. During December's very first Lysander sortie, a 'double' flown by McBride and Bathgate to Laon on the 10/11, Bathgate was shot down near Reims on the outward trip and was killed, together with his two passengers. It was never established whether he fell victim to flak or a night-fighter. McBride never reached his objective, turning back in the face of bad weather, and Stephen Hankey — flying a single trip to Compiegne — was also compelled to abandon for the same reason.

A Lysander sortie by Wing Commander Hodges on 15/16 December to Châtellerault also ended in failure, but for a different reason. During this period, several of 161 Squadron's Halifaxes were experimentally fitted with 'Gee', a position-fixing system that relayed electronic pulses from three ground stations to receiver equipment in the aircraft. The receiver measured the difference in time between the receipt of the ground signals, and converted the resulting information into terms of distance. Two sets of readings could then be plotted on a special chart known as a Gee Lattice Chart, and the point at which the two lines intersected was the receiver aircraft's position. Hodges, faced with a long trip into France in poor weather, had decided to install a Gee receiver in a Lysander and carry a navigator to operate it. Preliminary trials had gone well, but on the actual operation the Gee equipment interfered with the Lysander's compass and the sortie had to be abandoned.

The following night, 16/17 December, was the most tragic in the Squadron's history. Both the Halifaxes and Lysanders were operating when the weather suddenly clamped down, with the whole of southern England hidden under a blanket of low cloud and fog. Three Halifaxes were out that night (in fact, only fourteen Halifax sorties were flown during the month, together with nine Stirling) and their pilots found it impossible to land. With insufficient fuel to divert elsewhere, two of the pilots — Flight Lieutenant Gray and Flying Officer Harborow — tried to grope their way down through the fog, and both aircraft crash-landed. Gray was killed and all his crew were severely injured; Harborow's crew sustained fewer injuries, although they suffered one fatality, Flying Officer McMasters. The captain of the third Halifax, Warrant Officer Caldwell — realizing the hopelessness of the situation — ordered his crew to bale out and followed them into the darkness. All landed safely.

There were two Lysander sorties that night. On one of them, Bob Hodges reached Châtellerault on his second attempt (without trying to use Gee, this time) and scraped into Tangmere with two passengers on board, one of whom was Robin Hooper, mere minutes before the fog closed in completely.

For Stephen Hankey and 'McB', as his Squadron colleagues knew McBride, however, luck had run out. Returning from a double Lysander trip with passengers on board, they found Tangmere blanketed by fog. McBride tried to feel his way down, but crashed and burned; he lost his life, but the two passengers miraculously crawled out of the blazing wreck. Stephen Hankey decided to make for the airfield at Ford, a few miles away. While descending through cloud, he apparently lost control and his

N7280, one of the early batch of Lockheed Hudsons ordered for the RAF. N7263, the former King's Flight aircraft that served with No. 161 Squadron, was part of this batch.

An Armstrong Whitworth Whitley taking off. Whitleys bore the brunt of long-range special operations until replaced by the Halifax.

A single Martin Maryland, one of a batch originally intended for the French Air Force, served for a time with No. 161 Squadron and was evaluated for possible long-range SD operations. It was found unsuitable.

Douglas DB-7 light bombers, intended for the French, were taken over by the RAF to become the Boston I and II. The night-fighter version was known as the Havoc, and two such aircraft – BJ477 and AW399 – were used by No. 161 Squadron on 'Ascension' sorties.

Lysander spun into the ground. He and his two passengers were killed instantly.

So, on this ghastly note, No. 161 Squadron's year drew to a close. The loss of four Lysanders and four Halifaxes on operations (five Halifaxes, counting Gray's accident in November) had effectively halved the unit's strength, and the deaths of some of the Squadron's most experienced pilots was a physical blow to morale that would take time to overcome. Apart from that, both Squadron Leader Hugh Verity and Flying Officer Jimmy McCairns were now posted away, the former to take up a post as Air Liaison Officer (Operations) with HQ SOE in Baker Street, and the latter to Air Intelligence. For 161 Squadron, things would never be quite the same again.

5

No. 138 Squadron and the Polish Flight, 1943

The spring of 1943 saw a steady influx of Polish air and ground crews into No. 138 Squadron, the object being to train them alongside their RAF counterparts until they were ready to take their places in the new Polish Flight that was shortly to be formed under the command of Flight Lieutenant Stanislav Krol. Some of the personnel came from No. 301 (Pomeranian Polish) Squadron, which had been disbanded at Hemswell on 7 April 1943 after two and a half years of operations with No. 1 Bomber Group. No. 301 Squadron, which had operated Vickers Wellingtons, had a very distinguished record, and had suffered 203 casualties in the course of 1,260 sorties against enemy targets; to perpetuate its memory, it was decided to give the new special duties unit the unofficial designation of No. 301 Flight.

Squadron Leader Frank Griffiths, AFC, who commanded a flight of 138 Squadron in the summer of 1943, remembers the Poles as a 'magnificent headache'. Outwardly well disciplined, observing the courtesies of rank to the minutest detail, they would at the same time think nothing at all of lighting a cigarette in an aircraft saturated with the fumes from full petrol tanks and carrying a load of explosives. 'Rebuking a Pole', Griffiths recalls, 'was a waste of time. They would appear to understand, give a magnificent salute and then go away and default again.'

On one occasion, Griffiths — with Stanislav Krol interpreting — briefed two Polish crews to carry out some drops over France. Griffiths himself was to follow them across the Channel from Brighton to the estuary near le Crotoy, and then inland to the Forest of Crécy. Because there was a good deal of light flak on the French coast, the briefing stressed that the Halifaxes were to cross the Channel at wave-top height, climb quickly to 7,000 feet just short of the coast — out of range of the light flak — and then drop back to 250 feet over the Forest of Crécy.

The three aircraft took off one after the other, and as they crossed the Channel Squadron Leader Griffiths could clearly see the exhaust flames of the other Halifaxes ahead of him. When they reached the coast, however, to Griffiths' dismay the two Polish pilots made no attempt to gain height; instead, they raced in at low level, raking the enemy flak positions with their machine-guns. The result was predictable. Flying into the curtain of steel thrown up by the four-barrelled 20-mm guns, one of the Halifaxes crashed in a great balloon of fire. The second pilot was luckier; he managed to get away, but his aircraft was so badly damaged that he barely succeeded in getting home.[35]

This reckless spirit of aggression on the part of the Poles contributed in some measure to the growing losses sustained by 138 Squadron as 1943 wore on, but some of the most serious losses were sustained on operations over Holland, and these had nothing to do with the behaviour of the Poles. What SOE in London did not know was that since March 1942, the Abwehr had been infiltrating the network in Holland, and just over a year later had succeeded in setting up some thirty fake dropping zones. Captured Dutch agents were forced to send fake messages to SOE Headquarters, and although the agents took great pains to let SOE know that the messages were false — by omitting security code-words and so on — they were in fact accepted as genuine. By May 1943 the Germans had established eighteen radio links with SOE, with the result that almost every agent dropped by the RAF — together with considerable quantities of supplies — fell straight into enemy hands. The Luftwaffe night-fighters, too, were constantly on the prowl, for the Germans knew fairly accurately when the RAF aircraft were coming in and the idea was to shoot them down on the way to their objectives. It will never be known if night-fighters or flak accounted for the highest proportion of the special duties aircraft that went missing over Holland in the spring and summer of 1943, but in March and April of that year No. 138 Squadron alone lost six aircraft on operations.

Worse — much worse — was to come. With the Anglo-

American bombing offensive against Germany now well under way, the German anti-aircraft defences had reached a new peak of efficiency, thanks mainly to the efforts of General Josef Kammhuber, the dynamic commander of XII Fliegerkorps and the Luftwaffe's night-fighter force. Since his appointment in 1940 Kammhuber had striven to weld the German night defences into as efficient an organization as his resources would permit, and now, in the spring of 1943, he had five Geschwader (Wings) and four hundred twin-engined night-fighters under his command on bases ranging from Holland to the Mediterranean. These were controlled by a network of overlapping air-defence radar zones known as 'Himmelbett', stretching from north to south down the length of occupied Europe.

As long as the special duties aircraft could remain at low level they had a chance of escaping the watchful eyes of the enemy radar system, but on very long flights — to Poland and Czechoslovakia — this was not possible, for a piston-engined aircraft uses a lot of fuel when flying low, and on such trips the fuel margin was critical. Losses on Route One — the journey to central Europe over Denmark — grew alarmingly in the summer months of 1943, and the majority of the twelve 138 Squadron Halifaxes which failed to return in August and September of that year were operating along this route. The Squadron's losses reached an all-time high on 14 and 16 September, when seven out of sixteen Halifaxes sent to Poland were shot down and most of the others so seriously damaged that they were out of action for weeks. During this period the Squadron was left with only two serviceable aircraft, a situation that lasted until the arrival of three Liberators in October. Flown by Polish crews, these aircraft began operations almost immediately, following a newly-established route — Route Two — over southern Sweden; it was 120 miles longer than Route One, but infinitely safer.

The Liberator soon endeared itself to the crews who had been used to flying Halifaxes for so long. As well as having a greater range and load-carrying capacity, the Liberator was easier to jump from and was not so sensitive to icing or to a crosswind on take-off. It was also a far better aircraft from the point of view of comfort. Its main disadvantage lay in its engine exhaust system, which coughed out long blue flames that could be seen for miles at night, but as the Liberator had been originally intended for daylight operations the Americans had not considered it necessary to produce shielding for the exhausts, and so local modifications had to be carried out. The first two Liberator flights to Poland were made during the second half of October, both aircraft following Route Two over southern Sweden. The distance involved was 1,100 miles each way and the duration of the flights was fourteen and a half and sixteen hours respectively. Strong headwinds were encountered during both return trips and the aircraft just managed to struggle back to base, dangerously low on fuel.

It was some small consolation for the special duties crews, in the closing months of 1943, that they no longer had to rely entirely on map reading and dead reckoning to reach their objectives. Most aircraft were now equipped with a navigational radio aid known as 'Rebecca', which was used in conjunction with a small VHF radio transmitter on the ground. The transmitter, called 'Eureka', weighed about a hundred pounds; it was battery-powered and was activated by a signal from the aircraft's Rebecca equipment, enabling a navigator to home on to it from a range of between forty and seventy miles, depending on the aircraft's height. When both these instruments were properly used it was possible to guide an aircraft to its target with great accuracy, even to within fifty yards or so. They were also used for en-route navigation, Eureka beacons being planted at strategic points by members of the resistance. Two beacons, for example, were installed in the spires of cathedrals at Reims and Orleans, right in the middle of heavily-defended flak areas; from a height of 2,000 feet navigators could obtain their distance from these at over sixty miles range.

Unfortunately, many Resistance groups which received Eureka equipment either did not know how to use it properly or could not be bothered to use it at all, and consequently much of its effectiveness was lost. Many of the Eurekas air-dropped into the occupied territories were never heard of again, and there are no cases on record of Eureka/Rebecca and S-Phone being used in conjunction with one another to make accurate drops through cloud and haze, as was the original plan. Also, with some notable exceptions — such as the Eureka beacons at Reims and Orleans — the RAF's aim of establishing a network of powerful beacons across occupied Europe to aid navigation never came to fruition. However, the Rebecca/Eureka combination produced one useful result in that some Eurekas were set up in several remote areas, well away from concentrations of enemy troops, and manned on every night of the moon period each month. An aircraft that could not locate its objective, or carry out a drop over the primary target for any reason, could then fly to one of these 'depot grounds' and drop its load there. Nevertheless, relying on the Eurekas dotted around Europe became an increasingly risky business, especially after the Germans captured one and set up decoys.

In September 1943, following the landing of Allied forces in Italy, No. 138 Squadron's sphere of operations broadened considerably when, in view of the continual problem of range that beset the special duties aircraft, it was decided to detach flights of Halifaxes in rotation to Brindisi, some 280 miles southeast of Rome. An advance party with supporting equipment left Tempsford for this new location at the end of October, under the command of a Pole, Captain Oranowski.

Clandestine operations out of Brindisi, which for security reasons was known as No. 11 Base, were under the orders of an SOE officer, Lieutenant-Colonel Threlfall, but the administrative organization was somewhat complex. Although 138 Squadron's Polish personnel at Brindisi were now under the orders of Lieutenant-Colonel Threlfall, he in turn was subordinate to both the Polish section of SOE in London as far as administration was concerned and to General Stowell, the senior SOE officer in Italy, for air operations. Stowell, as well as being subordinate to SOE Headquarters in London, was also under the orders of General Maitland Wilson, the Supreme Allied Commander in the Mediterranean. To complicate matters still further, all operational flights from Brindisi came under the authority of Air Marshal Slessor, the RAF Commander-in-Chief in the Mediterranean and Middle East, who had a dual responsibility to the Air Staff in London and to General Maitland Wilson.

Nevertheless, the establishment of the base went ahead with considerable harmony during the closing weeks of 1943. While the organization was still under way, one of 138 Squadron's British-manned flights attempted several sorties to Poland, but without success; in each case, the Halifaxes had to turn back either with mechanical trouble or because of adverse weather. On 4 November the Squadron's Polish Flight was detached to Blida, near Algiers, because of overcrowding at Brindisi, and while it was based at this temporary location it received the Air Ministry designation of No. 1586 Flight, attached to No. 334 (Special Duties) Wing, although the Poles — for sentimental reasons — retained the unofficial designation of No. 301 Flight. In January 1944 the Flight returned to Brindisi, replacing the British flight of Halifaxes, which now returned to the United Kingdom.

The establishment of the special duties base at Brindisi meant that the dangerous Routes One and Two across Denmark and southern Sweden from Britain to eastern Europe could now be abandoned, and three new routes from Italy were set up. Route Three went across Lake Balaton in Hungary, passed to the west of Budapest and crossed the Tatra Mountains; on this route, the distance to Cracow from Brindisi was a little over 600 miles and to Warsaw 900. This was the best and most popular route but it had to be abandoned in April 1944, because as the Soviet armies advanced steadily westwards the Germans concentrated large anti-aircraft defences and numerous fighters in the Budapest/Balaton area. Route Four, slightly further east, went via Kotor in Yugoslavia, passed to the east of Budapest and then entered Poland east of the Tatras. Its length was similar to that of Route Three. Route Five, still further east, led directly to Lvov, a distance of 684 miles, via Durazzo in Albania and Bazias on the Yugoslav/Romanian border. On all three routes the aircraft flew high, between 10,000 and 11,500 feet, to avoid flak and — in the case of Route Three — to get over the Tatras safely.

Partly because of the re-organization, and partly because of bad weather, No. 138 Squadron's operations to eastern Europe were severely curtailed towards the end of 1943, and also in the first three months of 1944. There were no flights in November, three in December — carried out by the Polish Flight from Blida — and one each in January, February and March 1944. All of these were supply-dropping operations. The last agent-dropping sortie to eastern Europe had taken place on the night of 17/18 October 1943, from Tempsford, and over five months were to elapse before another sortie of this kind was carried out — from Brindisi — on 3 April 1944.

Many potential sorties were frustrated by violent weather, the pilots being forced to turn back in the face of storms, snow, heavy rain and fog. Also, Brindisi airfield had only one runway, which meant that operations often had to be cancelled when strong crosswinds were blowing. The Halifaxes — which were prone to 'weathercocking' in crosswind conditions — suffered most of all from this aspect; in the early hours of 6 January, 1944, two Halifaxes attempting to land at Brindisi in a strong crosswind crashed when they swung violently off the runway and they were written off.

Fortunately, the bitter winter was followed by a spell of exceptionally fine spring weather that enabled the special duties crews to work off the substantial backlog of supplies that had accumulated during the previous months. In April, the Poles alone flew 100 separate operations, visiting five or six objectives in the course of a single sortie to Poland and the Balkans, and in May the figure was 138. It was as though the crews knew that they were on the last lap, that this year of 1944 would see the end of Germany's domination of Europe. It was perhaps as well that they could not know that, for the special duties squadrons, the sternest test and the greatest sacrifices were yet to come.

6

No. 161 Squadron Operations, 1944-45

Back at Tempsford, bad weather prevailed throughout January 1944, making it impossible for either 138 or 161 Squadrons to utilize the moon period fully. No. 161's Halifaxes flew twenty-two sorties, three of them during the dark period, but crews found great difficulty in locating their receptions and only a few trips were successful. There was an unfortunate incident at the close of the moon period, on 23 January, when two Halifaxes piloted by Flying Officer Smith and Flight Sergeant Robertson took off from Tempsford at 11.30 on an air-sea rescue detail; both aircraft were due back at 16.30, but they failed to return and no trace of them was ever found. Both crews had just completed their training, and this was their first operation.

Nine Stirlings — six from No. 214 Squadron, two from No. 199 and one from No. 149 — were attached to Tempsford during January, under the command of Squadron Leader Jeffries, and these aircraft flew a total of twenty sorties, only a handful of which were successful. The Lysanders, partly because of the weather but also because of a shortage of aircraft following December's tragedies, did not operate at all.

The first pickup operation of 1944 was made by a Hudson on the night of 4/5 February, when Squadron Leader Len Ratcliff — commanding 'C' Flight, in which all 161's Hudsons were now grouped — flew to Angers with one passenger and brought out eight. The real purpose of this trip was to bring back an agent named Henri Déricourt to London for interrogation; he was suspected of being a double agent, for several receptions organized by him had resulted in the arrest of operatives by the enemy. Déricourt did not in fact return to England on this occasion, but he did fly out by Lysander a few days later.[36]

Of two Lysander sorties organized for the night of 4/5 February, only one — a 'double' flown by two of 161's new pilots, Flight Lieutenants Whitaker and Anderson — was a success, five agents being landed in the Issoudun area and three picked up. The other Lysander pilot, Flying Officer McDonald, called off his operation when he failed to sight his reception. This was also the reason for the failure of a second Hudson sortie that night, flown to Chalon-sur-Saône by Flying Officer John Affleck.

Affleck, however, had his fair share of excitement on the night of 8/9 February, when he took a Hudson to Villevieux to collect four passengers. These included Flight Lieutenant J.F.Q. Brough (who had been on the run in France since his 138 Squadron Halifax had been shot down on the night of 3/4 November 1943), agent Raymond Aubrac, his wife and their young son. The field was badly waterlogged, and as Affleck was taxying to the take-off point the aircraft became bogged down. The pilot and his crew climbed down and explained the position to the reception committee and their passengers. Affleck told them that by his reckoning, they had about ninety minutes in which to free the aircraft. If they had not got it clear of the mud at the end of that time they would have to set fire to it to prevent it falling into enemy hands. He warned them that the aircraft's engines had already created enough racket to awaken the dead, and with a German army garrison only three miles away it was quite possible that enemy troops were already on their way to the landing ground.

All hands immediately set to work to try and push the aircraft clear, but it was hopeless. The Hudson was too heavy, and by this time its rear fuselage had sunk to ground level. As well as all the other problems that confronted him, Affleck was growing increasingly worried about the condition of Aubrac and his wife; she was eight months pregnant, and showing signs that the birth might not be far away. An incredibly brave woman, only a few days earlier she had helped to rescue her husband at gunpoint from a Gestapo van that was taking him to the condemned cell. His captivity must have been a terrible ordeal, for he was weak and looked on the verge of total collapse.

Suddenly, there was an alarm as dark shapes were seen moving stealthily through the trees that bordered the field. The scare, however, was soon over. The newcomers were inhabitants of a nearby village, who had been alerted by the noise and had come to see what was going on. As best he could, Affleck explained the situation to them and someone went off to fetch horses and oxen. These were quickly harnessed to the Hudson while the Frenchmen set to work with picks and shovels, digging trenches away from the wheels of the aircraft under the careful supervision of the pilot, who was anxious in case their over-enthusiasm might cause some damage.

After an hour — during which time there was another scare when a German aircraft flew low overhead — all the effort was rewarded. The horses and oxen gave a last heave and the Hudson came free with a gigantic sucking sound. Affleck lost no time in climbing aboard and restarting the engines, which he used to take the aircraft clear of the boggy patch. Then, with his passengers safely inside, he taxied cautiously round the field, turned into wind and gave the engines full throttle.

The first take-off attempt was a failure, the mud-caked Hudson refusing to gain flying speed. Affleck taxied back to the take-off point, becoming briefly bogged on the way, and tried again. Halfway down the field, he felt with sickening certainty that he was not going to make it. The Hudson's take-off speed was ninety knots, and with the trees on the far boundary rushing closer the airspeed indicator showed only fifty knots. Then the miracle happened; the Hudson hit a bump and lurched into the air. Somehow it kept flying, teetering on the edge of a stall while Affleck took it over the treetops with only feet to spare. He realized that he had been stranded in France for two and a half hours.

Despite the fact that his radio aerials had been torn off in the struggle to free the aircraft, and that consequently he had no means of using his IFF to alert the British air defences of his approach, Affleck landed safely at Tempsford and disembarked his passengers, all of whom were frozen, soaked through and covered in mud. Madame Aubrac was immediately rushed by ambulance to Queen Charlotte's Hospital in London, where she gave birth to a baby girl only a few hours later. For his exploit in bringing the aircraft home safely, Affleck was promoted to Flight Lieutenant and awarded an immediate DSO.

His was not the only pickup sortie that night. There were two others, one of them a double Lysander. This was flown by Flight Lieutenant Anderson and Flying Officer McDonald, who landed at a field south-east of Paris to drop four passengers and collect four more. The other Lysander sortie was flown by Flight Lieutenant Whitaker, who went to Angers to land two passengers and bring out two — the latter being Henri Déricourt and his wife.

An abortive Lysander sortie on 10 February was followed by another 'double' on the night of the 11/12. This was flown by Flying Officers McDonald and Bell, the latter a newcomer to the Squadron, and was a tragic failure. The two aircraft made rendezvous in poor visibility over their target field at Vierzon and McDonald went down to land first. He made two attempts, overshooting each time, and on the third attempt Bell, circling overhead, saw his aircraft tip over and burst into flames. It was later confirmed that McDonald had been killed and laid to rest in the churchyard at Farge-en-Septaine, but it was believed that his two passengers had escaped. Bell, realizing that it would be futile to try and land after the accident, returned to base with his passengers on board.

Two more pickup attempts in February — one a Lysander on 11/12 by Flight Lieutenant Whitaker and the other a Hudson on 15/16 by Wing Commander Hodges — failed because of bad weather, which also severely restricted operations by 161 Squadron's four-engined aircraft. The Halifaxes flew thirty-one sorties during the moon period, while six Stirlings on attachment from 149 Squadron at Lakenheath carried out twenty-six.

March 1944 saw a change of command, with Wing Commander Alan Boxer posted in from Air Ministry (A12(c)) as CO. Squadron Leader G. de G. Sells moved in to take over the Lysanders of 'A' Flight from Robin Hooper, who was given the acting rank of Wing Commander and posted to Air Ministry Intelligence.

A general improvement in the weather during March led to an overall increase in the tempo of operations, the Halifaxes flying seventy-one sorties. The Hudson Flight, commanded by Squadron Leader Ratcliff, received an injection of eight new crews, all drawn from Coastal Command; unfortunately, two pilots were found unsuitable for special duties operations and had to be replaced. There was one tragic incident on 28 March, when Hudson IIIA FK767, piloted by Flying Officer Baughan, crashed and burned while on a night-flying exercise with the loss of all its crew. The Hudsons carried out no pickup operations during March (or during April, for that matter) being engaged exclusively on 'Ascension' work or on supply-dropping trials.

The Squadron ORB records seven Lysander pickups during the month, of which five were successful. (According to Hugh Verity, there was an eighth, flown by an unknown pilot to Baudreville on behalf of SIS on the night of the 2/3.) The first recorded trip, however, also carried out on this night, was flown by Flight Lieutenant Anderson to Vatan, where he landed two passengers and collected two more.

There were two double Lysander sorties on the night of 3/4 March, one to Châteauroux and the other to a field twenty miles south of Bourges. The former sortie was flown by Flying Officer Bell and a new member of the Squadron, Lieutenant Hysing-Dahl, a Norwegian. The latter landed two passengers and picked up two more, returning safely to Tangmere, but there was no news of Bell. What had happened was that the engine of Bell's Lysander had failed over Normandy and he had been forced down near Plumetot, wrecking the aircraft on landing and cutting his face and leg quite badly. His two passengers escaped with bruising; all three were sheltered by the local Resistance, who saw the agents on their way and arranged for Bell to be flown home by Lysander a few nights later. The second Lysander sortie that night, carried out by Flight Lieutenants Anderson and Whitaker, was a complete success, the two pilots landing four agents and bringing out six. The same two pilots were airborne again on 6/7 March, flying to Compiegne with two outbound passengers and another six on the homeward run, and it was Anderson who — on a single Lysander operation on the night of 13/14 March — went to a strip near Angers with two passengers and collected four, one of whom was Bell.

A sortie by Lieutenant Hysing-Dahl to Issoudun on 15/16 March had to be abandoned because of cloud and fog, but on the last night of the month the Norwegian successfully completed another operation to the same location, landing one agent and picking up two. On that same night, Anderson and

Whitaker flew a successful 'double' to Touraine, exchanging five passengers for five more.

The Halifaxes of 'B' Flight once again flew seventy-one sorties during April 1944. One aircraft, LK738, piloted by Flight Sergeant McGibbon, failed to return from operations on the night of the 10/11.

Another 161 Squadron aircraft that failed to return in April, under much more curious circumstances, was a Hudson that took off on a cross-country flight across Wales and Cornwall. Days later, the news came that it had landed at Gothenburg, in Sweden, and that the crew was safe. It seemed that both the pilot and navigator had been guilty of some serious errors and had flown off on a north-easterly heading, instead of a north-westerly one; the pilot thought the water he was flying over was the Irish Sea, when in fact it was the Baltic, and by that time it was too late to do anything about it, because his fuel was running low. He landed the Hudson on the first airfield that appeared ahead — which fortunately turned out to be in neutral Sweden — and was interned, together with his crew.[37]

Two double and one single Lysander sorties were flown on the night of 5/6 April, but on this occasion the old duo of Anderson and Whitaker were unable to sight any reception and consequently returned to base. The second double was a success, four agents being landed in the Touraine area by Flight Lieutenant Bill Taylor and another pilot and six brought back. The single sortie was flown by Per Hysing-Dahl, who picked up three passengers from a strip near Chartres.

Three single Lysander operations were carried out on the night of 9/10 April, and all of them were successfully completed. Flight Lieutenant Anderson landed three agents south of Bourges and picked up another three, while Flight Lieutenant Bob Large — making his first pickup — exchanged one for one at a field to the east of Angers. Flight Lieutenant Taylor undertook the third sortie, dropping three passengers at a point near Châteauroux and collecting three more.

Flight Lieutenant George Turner set out on a 'double' with Per Hysing-Dahl on 11/12 April, the two pilots flying to a strip half a mile north of Outarville to drop off four passengers and bring out seven between them. The month's pickup operations closed with two 'doubles', the first flown by Flight Lieutenant

Taylor and Squadron Leader Ratcliff on the 28/29; on this occasion Bill Taylor experienced engine trouble and was forced to turn back, but Ratcliff carried on to land three agents at Châteauroux, bringing out five large packages. Châteauroux was again the objective for the month's last 'double', when Flight Lieutenant Bob Large and Flying Officer Alcock delivered three passengers and collected two on 30 April. Large's Lysander was slightly damaged by flak on the homeward trip and ground-looped on landing because of a burst tyre, but he and his passenger escaped unhurt. The passenger was the famous Violette Szabo.[38]

May 1944 was a month of great excitement and anticipation, for hardly anyone could fail to be aware that the Allied invasion of Europe was only weeks, perhaps even days away. No. 161 Squadron's Halifaxes flew fifty-five sorties in the course of the month and the Hudsons played their part too, carrying out twelve air-drops over various targets on the Continent as well as making nineteen 'Ascension' sorties. One Hudson, 'Q', piloted by Flight Lieutenant Hale, was shot down over Tilburg in Holland on the last night of the month, he and the other two members of his crew being killed. It was the first 161 Squadron Hudson to be lost on operations.

It was a Hudson, flown by John Affleck, that made the first pickup of the month, taking eight passengers to an unnamed airfield in France and bringing out eight more. Two Lysander operations were also flown that night (3/4 May); the first was a success, Per Hysing-Dahl unloading two passengers and collecting two, but the second ended in disaster. Flight Lieutenant Leslie Whitaker apparently strayed over an enemy airfield, where he was shot down and killed. The French buried him at Etampes.

On 6/7 May, Flying Officer G.J.F. Alexander carried a load of equipment to Outarville and brought out three passengers. One of them was Major Walker Mahurin, an American fighter ace of the 56th Fighter Group who had notched up twenty-four 'kills' while flying P-47 Thunderbolts before being shot down on an escort mission.[39]

On the night of 7/8 May, another newcomer to the Squadron, Flight Lieutenant E.A.G.C. Bruce, flew to Angers to exchange two passengers, while on the following night

103

Squadron Leader Ratcliff, Flight Lieutenant Large and Lieutenant Hysing-Dahl carried out a treble Lysander operation (the first in eight months), landing six passengers in Touraine and bringing home eight. Only one more pickup operation was attempted in May, on the 10/11; this was flown by another new pilot, Pilot Officer Newhouse, and was abandoned when the pilot failed to sight his reception.

Three Lysander pickup operations were mounted in June, all of them on the night of the 2/3 and all successful. Flight Lieutenant Taylor went to Estrées St Denis with two passengers and returned with three; Flight Lieutenant Turner landed at an unrecorded destination with three and collected one, while Flying Officer Alexander went to Outarville with one passenger on the outward trip and three on the homeward. Otherwise, for this historic month of the invasion, No. 161 Squadron's ORB shows that the Halifaxes of 'B' Flight flew sixty-four sorties, thirty-four of them in the dark period, doubtless to supply the Resistance workers who were now carrying out acts of sabotage in growing numbers behind the enemy lines in support of the Allied ground forces. Meanwhile, the 'Ascension' Hudsons had an unlucky month; out of ten attempts to establish new contacts, only four were successful.

Good weather over the United Kingdom during the moon period of July was not matched by conditions over France and the Low Countries; nevertheless, the Halifaxes made eighty-two sorties, and during the latter part of the month a shuttle service was organized between Tempsford and Blida in North Africa, the Halifaxes dropping supplies on both the outward and homeward runs. The operation was not particularly successful, mainly because of weather conditions over the target areas. 'B' Flight began conversion to Short Stirlings during July, two or three crews going over to 138 Squadron, which had priority in re-equipping with this type.

The Hudsons of 'C' Flight made eleven sorties, including three pickups, but their record was marred by the loss of Hudson 'R' which went missing over Holland on the night of the 5/6 July. This aircraft, piloted by Flight Lieutenant Menzies, also carried four agents, who were presumed to have been killed along with the crew. Hudsons made thirteen 'Ascension' sorties during the month, of which seven were successful.

Flight Lieutenant John Affleck made the first pickup of the month, flying to an unspecified location in France in one of the Hudsons with eight passengers each way on the night of 5/6 July; he had already made the attempt on 3/4 July, but had called off the operation when no reception was sighted.

The first Lysander operation of July — a 'double' to a field near Chenonceaux, flown by Turner and Hysing-Dahl — ended in disaster for the latter pilot and his passengers. Turner found the field all right and made his exchange of passengers, but Hysing-Dahl failed to do so and turned back for the coast with his three passengers still on board. The Normandy beach-head area was stiff with Allied anti-aircraft guns, and pilots had to stick to a narrow corridor near Trouville in order to be safe. Hysing-Dahl, however, strayed off course and found himself over the beach-head, where his Lysander came under heavy fire and was badly hit in the oil reservoir and one wing. A fragment of shrapnel wounded the pilot in one hand, and a few moments later the engine seized, starved of oil.

With shells still bursting all around him, Per Hysing-Dahl glided down towards the dark waters of the Channel, turning the Lysander so that he could see the moon's reflection in the water. The Lysander's fixed undercarriage ploughed into the surface and the aircraft flipped over on to its back with a force that threw the three passengers out of the rear cockpit. Hysing-Dahl undid his straps and extricated himself from the sinking aircraft with some difficulty, kicking his way to the surface and inflating his personal seat dinghy (his Mae West lifejacket would not inflate). He spotted the three passengers struggling in the water and managed to get two of them into the dinghy, but the third drowned before the pilot could help him.

Hysing-Dahl and the two remaining passengers were eventually picked up by an American motor torpedo boat after spending four hours in the water. Some time after they were taken on board this vessel, there was a further tragedy; another of Hysing-Dahl's French passengers died, apparently from shock, for he had received no visible injury. The Norwegian pilot and the sole surviving passenger were brought ashore safely. It was Per Hysing-Dahl's last operation with 161 Squadron; in August, he was posted to Headquarters, Royal Norwegian Air Force. He survived the war, and later became a member of the Norwegian Parliament.

Also on the night of 7/8 July, Flight Lieutenant Taylor — with Flight Sergeant Thomas in the rear cockpit — carried out a mail pickup from a location in France. The Lysander did not land, but flew low over the field trailing a hook, which engaged with a line suspended between two poles. Thomas's job was to winch in this line, at the end of which was a mail bag. The trip was successful and 161 Squadron carried out a number of sorties of this kind before Lysander operations ceased.

The last pickup of July was made in the dark period by a Hudson, flown by Wing Commander Boxer, who was making his first trip of this kind. On the night of the 27/28 he landed on the disused airfield of Le Blanc, near Poitiers, to disembark two passengers and bring out four, all of them evading aircrew.

In August the Lysander Flight moved to Winkleigh, near Exeter, and continued its operations from there. Two mail pickups were carried out in the course of the moon period. Personnel pickups began on the night of 4/5 August, when there were three Lysander operations, two of them doubles; unfortunately, one of the latter ended in tragedy. Flying Officers Peter Arkell and J.P. Alcock were flying to Vallon, south of the Loire, when Arkell saw his companion's Lysander go down in flames ahead of him. Arkell went on to complete the operation, landing two passengers and collecting three. The other double that night was carried out by Flying Officers Newhouse and Alexander, who went to La Chartre sur Loire to land five passengers and bring out five, one of them a girl with a broken hip. The field was quite unsuitable and Alexander damaged his aircraft on landing. He managed to get airborne and make a dangerous and difficult flight home with no radio aids and a control column that would not move forwards or backwards, which forced him to use the trimmer to control climb and descent. To add to his problems, he was shot at by light flak, and when he reached the English coast he found a blanket of fog underneath him. He headed for St Merryn, in Cornwall, which was equipped with FIDO fog dispersal gear, and found the airfield fortunately lit up. He landed downwind, narrowly missing four Liberators which were taking off in the opposite direction, left his aircraft on the perimeter track — the damage it had sustained preventing him from steering it — and set off to

106

find assistance. He walked around the airfield perimeter for an hour before he eventually found flying control, where — since he was wearing civilian clothes — he caused some consternation before he identified himself.

The single Lysander operation that was flown that night was a failure, the pilot — Flying Officer Lamberton — returning to base to report that he had sighted no reception. His operation was completed on 5/6 August by Squadron Leader Ratcliff, who delivered two passengers and brought back one. Flight Lieutenant George Turner was also airborne on this night, landing one agent in the Touraine area and picking up three. There was only one more Lysander pickup attempt in August, when Flight Lieutenant Bill Taylor flew to Les Andelys but failed to find his target field in poor visibility.

Otherwise, August 1944 was very much the month of 161 Squadron's Hudsons, which undertook six pickups, three of them doubles. The first of these was flown on the night of the 6/7 by Wing Commander A.H.C. Boxer and Flying Officer H.B. Ibbott, who flew to a location near Poitiers with eleven troops of the crack Special Air Service, charged with the task of operating behind the enemy lines alongside the French Forces of the Interior. They also carried several cases of small arms and ammunition. The two Hudsons brought home twenty passengers between them.

There was a single Hudson pickup operation on the night of 7/8 August, when Squadron Leader Wilkinson took four passengers into France and brought out an exceptional load of thirteen. On 10/11 July, Wing Commander Boxer and Flight Lieutenant John Affleck delivered thirteen passengers to different French locations, returning with four passengers and some packages, and then there was a gap until the night of 31 August/1 September, when a double was flown by Wing Commander Boxer and Flight Lieutenant Helfer and another by Squadron Leader Wilkinson and Flying Officer Ibbott. These four aircraft took fourteen passengers to France between them, but brought only four home.

The Halifaxes of 'B' Flight carried out sixty-eight sorties during August and achieved a respectable success rate, but only at the price of three aircraft which failed to return from operations. Flight Lieutenant Loos went missing on the night of

5/6, Flight Sergeant Nichols on 9/10, and Flight Lieutenant Green on 28/29. As the month closed, the Squadron was preparing to re-equip with Stirlings; No. 138 was already using these aircraft, and four crews from that unit were attached to No. 161 to finish their tours of operations on Halifaxes.

With Allied forces now in control of most of France and pushing ahead into Belgium, operations by 161 Squadron's Hudsons and Lysanders during September were devoted mainly to special transport duties, carrying mail and passengers to the continental headquarters of the Allied armies. The Hudsons carried out sixty-five of these trips and the Lysanders twenty-three; unfortunately, one Lysander pilot, Flying Officer Lamberton, failed to return to Tempsford on a routine flight from Le Bourget and was not heard of again.

The last two 161 Squadron pickups were both doubles and were flown on the night of 5/6 September by — appropriately — Group Captain 'Mouse' Fielden, Flight Lieutenant Terence Helfer, Wing Commander Boxer and Flying Officer A.N. Ferris, who landed twelve passengers and some stores and also carried twelve passengers on the homeward run. Apart from a shaky landing by Boxer, who had some difficulty in avoiding a group of people who were clustered near the touchdown point, and the failure of Fielden to locate his target in poor visibility — compelling him to divert to Brussels — these sorties were completed without incident. It was something of an anti-climactic close to two and a half years of pickup work.

Three Halifax sorties were flown by 'B' Flight before these aircraft were finally exchanged for Stirlings, and the latter made twenty sorties in September — although nine of these were daylight operations to drop supplies to Allied forces in Belgium, who were racing ahead in their desperate attempt to join up with the British 1st Airborne Division at Arnhem. Seven 'Ascension' sorties were also flown by the Hudsons before this type of work was suspended, although the suspension turned out to be only temporary. 'Ascension' sorties were again flown in October, the Hudsons involved registering five successes out of nine operations.

There were very few operations in October 1944, mainly because of adverse weather. The Stirlings made eight sorties and one aircraft, piloted by Squadron Leader Abecassis, failed to return from a mission to Denmark. The fate of this aircraft is not recorded, but it seems to have diverted to Sweden for some reason, as the Squadron ORB notes that some members of the crew wrote home from that country. One other Stirling (Flight Lieutenant Levy) was lost in a flying accident, the aircraft breaking up in mid-air and crashing near Potton, two miles from Tempsford. There were no survivors. The Hudson Flight was busy throughout the month transporting medical supplies to France and Belgium, although two operational parachute drops were carried out, and the Lysanders — now non-operational in Britain at least — were engaged in ferry work.

Poor weather prevailed during November, but the Stirlings managed thirty-five sorties to Denmark and Holland. The Lysander Flight was now disbanded, although three aircraft were retained on strength for the time being, and the Hudsons were redesignated 'A' Flight. They carried out six operations during the month, of which three were successful. There was a serious loss on the night of 26/27 November, when the flight commander, Squadron Leader Reg Wilkinson, failed to return from an agent-dropping trip over Germany. It was later learned that his Hudson had been shot down three miles north-east of Houffalize, in Belgium, and the crew of four killed.

With the exception of those being retrained for other duties, the Lysander pilots of the former 'A' Flight were posted elsewhere early in December, a month that saw twenty-two sorties by the Squadron's Stirling aircraft. Five of these were 'spoofs' carried out in conjunction with the radio countermeasures aircraft of No. 100 Group, and involved the dropping of 'Window' in support of the Allied counter-offensive in the Ardennes, where the Germans had smashed through a sector of the American lines in what was to become known as the 'Battle of the Bulge'. Four Hudson operations were laid on during the moon period, of which two were successful, agents being dropped into Germany. 'Ascension' sorties continued, contacts now being established with contacts inside German territory.

Appalling weather during January 1945 brought flying to a virtual standstill, and the situation was little better in February. During this month the 'Ascension' sorties finally came to an end, having contributed much to the overall effort of SOE. There was a very unfortunate incident during the month, when a Mustang of the USAAF made a dummy attack on Stirling LK236 'Y', piloted by Flying Officer Timperley, while the latter was in the Tempsford circuit; the Mustang collided with the Stirling, shearing off the bomber's tail unit. None of the crew survived.

The weather improved somewhat in March and there were sixty-five sorties by 161's Stirlings, together with seventeen agent-dropping trips by the Hudsons of 'A' Flight, one of them to Norway. It was tragic that this month, so close to the end of the war in Europe, should witness the Squadron's heaviest-ever losses; three Stirlings and three Hudsons failed to return from operations. One Stirling (Wing Commander Brogan, DFC) was lost over Denmark; the others were shot down over the Low Countries. The three Hudson losses all occurred on the same night, 20/21 March 1945. One aircraft, flown by Flight Lieutenant Chris Ragan, was shot down over Germany en route to its target and all four crew members killed; the second, piloted by Flight Lieutenant Bob Ferris, had just dropped its agent to the east of Remagen when it was shot down on the homeward run over France; and the third, with Flight Lieutenant Terence Helfer as its captain, was destroyed over Belgium. Only Helfer survived, being thrown clear and descending under his parachute with severe lacerations and burns. There is a strong possibility that all three Hudsons were shot down by Allied night intruders, which over the past few weeks had been a far more serious menace to the special duties aircraft than enemy night-fighters.

It was almost the end. Before March closed, No. 161 Squadron was transferred from the operational control of No. 3 Group to HQ No. 38 Group Fighter Command. This administrative change broke up the long association with No. 138 Squadron, which now moved to Tuddenham in Suffolk and reverted to main force operations. Re-equipped with Lancasters, No. 138 flew 105 sorties on nine bombing missions before the end of the war, after which it dropped food supplies into Holland and was engaged in repatriating prisoners to the United Kingdom.

No. 161 Squadron persevered doggedly through April, flying seventy-two Stirling sorties and seventeen Hudson. One aircraft, Stirling FK763, was lost in the course of the month, crashing near Dorking, but the pilot — Flight Lieutenant Webb — and his crew baled out safely. During April there was a scheme to replace the ageing Hudsons with North American Mitchells and one aircraft was in fact taken on charge, being suitably modified for agent-dropping operations. However, the end of the European War brought about an end to these plans, and it was the Squadron's Stirling and Hudson aircraft which, during May 1945, carried out the final wartime tasks of supply and repatriation. The Squadron disbanded at Tempsford on 2 June 1945.

7

Operation Carpetbagger: USAAF Clandestine Operations, 1943-45

The United States Army Air Force's contribution to clandestine air operations over Europe really began in August 1943, following the disbandment of the 4th and 22nd Anti-Submarine Squadrons of the 479th Anti-Submarine Group. The aircrews and some of the aircraft — Consolidated B-24 Liberators — belonging to these units were placed in reserve by Lieutenant-General Ira Eaker, commanding the 8th USAAF in England, and they were used to form the initial complement of the 36th and 406th Bombardment Squadrons when the latter were activated on 11 November 1943 and attached to the 482nd Bombardment Group (Pathfinder) at Alconbury.

These two squadrons, the USAAF's original 'Carpetbaggers', had much the same brief as their RAF counterparts at Tempsford, in other words the dropping of supplies and agents into occupied Europe. Crew training — with the assistance of the Royal Air Force — went ahead during the closing weeks of 1943 and on the night of 4/5 January 1944 the 'Carpetbaggers' carried out their first supply drop over France, operating out of Tempsford on this occasion. During the next three months they would go on to complete 213 out of 268 attempted sorties, most of them to supply Resistance groups in France north of the Loire.

Some organizational changes in February and March 1944 resulted in the 'Carpetbagger' squadrons moving to Watton, in Norfolk, where they were assigned to the 8th Air Force Composite Command and came under the operational control of the 801st Bombardment Group, commanded by Lieutenant-Colonel Clifford J. Heflin. At the end of May the two original

'Carpetbagger' squadrons were joined by two more, the 788th and 850th, in anticipation of the greater demands that would have to be met following the Allied invasion of Normandy, and the four squadrons moved to Harrington in Lincolnshire, close to the coast of East Anglia. Their total strength now was forty B-24s.

The Liberators assigned to clandestine work were stripped of all anti-submarine and bombing equipment and were fitted with Rebecca and S-Phone for communications with operatives on the other side of the Channel. Each B-24 had its ball turret removed and replaced by a metal shroud, which was fitted into the opening to form a 'Joe Hole' for the despatch of agents by parachute. Other modifications included a plywood fuselage floor covering to provide more comfort for the occupants and also to facilitate movement, the provision of blackout curtains for the waist gun ports, perspex blisters for the pilot's and co-pilot's side windows to afford greater downward visibility, and separate compartments for the navigator and bombardier. Waist and nose guns were removed, and the aircraft were painted matt black overall.

The B-24s of the four 'Carpetbagger' squadrons flew on 28 nights during July 1944, dropping 4,680 containers, 2,909 packages, 1,378 bundles of leaflets and 62 agents in 397 sorties. Some of the trips were made in weather which, by normal 8th Air Force standards, would have been classed as unflyable.

Further administrative changes in August led to the 801st Bombardment Group being renumbered the 492nd Bombardment Group, while its four squadrons became the 856th, 857th, 858th and 859th. Fewer operations were carried out during this month, since much of the operational area covered by the 'Carpetbaggers' was now in Allied hands, and the occupation of most of the remainder of France in September brought a cessation of full-scale supply and agent drops, the Americans flying their last missions on the night of 16/17 September.

The 492nd Group had four C-47 (Dakota) aircraft at its disposal, and on 8 July one of these landed at a field in occupied France to deliver stores and evacuate passengers. During the five weeks that followed the C-47s made 25 sorties to 12 different locations, delivering 62 tons of arms and ammunition, flying in

76 passengers and evacuating 213. The last of these sorties was carried out on 18 August.

With the completion of full-scale supply operations in September the 492nd Bombardment Group became engaged in delivering fuel and equipment to the Allied forces on the Continent, and also carried out a number of medium-level night bombing operations, which for the Americans was a considerable departure from normal operational procedure. Only one of the 492nd's four squadrons, the 856th, was held ready for further 'Carpetbagger' operations, and the Group's four C-47s were attached to it for the evacuation of Allied PoWs from a central assembly point near Annecy.

The 856th, in fact, virtually became an autonomous unit within the 8th Air Force, being directly responsible now to the Office of Strategic Services (OSS), the American equivalent of SOE. However, little in the way of clandestine operations seems to have come its way during the closing weeks of 1944; the only recorded sorties involved two Liberator flights to Holland, one to Norway and two to Denmark before the end of the year.

Nevertheless, between 1 January and 5 March 1945 the 856th completed forty-one sorties to these countries, after which — on 14 March — it was returned to the operational control of the 492nd Bombardment Group. One of the latter's squadrons, the 859th, had left for Italy in December, and the other three were now made available for both special duties work and bombing operations.

On 9 March 1945, aircraft of the 856th and 858th Squadrons were detached to Dijon, from which base they dropped agents over Germany in a series of operations that lasted until 26 April. An interesting point is that, during these operations over Germany, two Mosquito aircraft based at Dijon (and sometimes Lyons) carried out a series of sorties under the code-name 'Red Stocking'. Similar to No. 161 Squadron's 'Ascension' sorties, these were designed to establish contact with operatives inside Germany. The crews of the Mosquitos were USAAF, but it is not clear from the records whether the aircraft involved were Canadian-built Mosquitos supplied to the USAAF under the designation F-8, or whether they were on loan from the RAF. Meanwhile, the rest of the 'Carpetbaggers' at Harrington continued to concentrate their efforts on Denmark and Norway;

in the latter case, small parties of Norwegian-speaking commandos were dropped in the interior, doubtless with the object of causing havoc behind the enemy lines should an invasion of Norway prove necessary.

In the event, it did not. When the German forces in Europe capitulated on 8 May 1945, the total number of sorties attempted by the 'Carpetbaggers' in thirteen months of operations stood at 2,857, of which 1,860 had been successful; 20,495 containers and 11,174 packages had been despatched to the various Resistance movements, and a thousand agents dropped. The cost to the 'Carpetbaggers', from January 1944 to May 1945, was twenty-four Liberators lost on operations, and a further eight so badly damaged that they had to be written off. Two hundred and eight aircrew were killed or posted missing, although many of the latter eventually turned up safe and well, having escaped by parachute.

The overall USAAF effort to supply partisans in Europe, however, was on a much vaster scale of operations than those mounted by the 'Carpetbagger' squadrons. Shortly after D-Day, 6 June 1944, Supreme Headquarters Allied Expeditionary Force received intelligence that the 'Maquis', the French Forces of the Interior, already controlled four of the country's Departments and were fighting hard for control of several others. The total number of armed Maquis thought to be involved in the fighting was sixteen thousand, but SHAEF Intelligence believed that a further thirty-one thousand were ready to enter the battle if arms and ammunition could be delivered to them — and the total number of FFI engaged might even rise to a hundred thousand if, following French successes in the field, other recruits joined the cause.

By extending the range of their operations to Châteauroux and the Cantal area, south-east of Limoges, the four 'Carpetbagger' squadrons of the 42nd Bombardment Group could theoretically keep about thirteen thousand Maquis supplied with arms and ammunition in south central France, but this was by no means enough. With a massive increase in air supply deliveries, it seemed possible that the FFI could establish complete control of all southern France, and even with partial control the Maquisards could seriously disrupt enemy communications, divert troops from the vital Normandy sector and create safe dropping zones for Allied airborne forces taking part in the invasion of the south, which was scheduled for August.

This could only be achieved by diverting heavy bombers from normal operations. SHAEF's estimate was that by laying on an extra 340 supply-dropping sorties a month, with the aid of B-17 bombers diverted from other duties, an additional thirty-four thousand FFI troops could be maintained in the field. It was too good an opportunity to miss. Consequently, on 15 June 1944, at SHAEF's request, the 8th Air Force indicated its readiness to divert seventy-five B-17s on to supply-dropping tasks, and three days later the total number of aircraft promised was raised to between a hundred and eighty and three hundred. The task was allotted to the 3rd Air Division, which assigned five bomber wings of thirty-six aircraft each. While Special Forces Headquarters assembled loaded containers at the various airfields involved, laid on signals and communications procedures with the FFI and selected target areas in the sectors that were most in need of supply, the 3rd Air Division's crews received hasty training in 'Carpetbagger' methods in readiness for their coming task.

The target areas jointly selected after consultation between SHAEF, 8th Air Force and OSS lay in the Department of Haute-Savoie, where FFI supplies were at a desperately low level after days of bitter fighting that had resulted in the French gaining control of almost the whole region by 18 June; the mountainous Ain area to the west of Geneva, which had been almost liberated by the Maquis when, on 14 June, shortage of supplies and ammunition had compelled the French to fall back; the area south-east of Dijon, where the FFI was hard at work disrupting enemy traffic and communications; the region south-east of Limoges, where an uprising by the Maquis had brought enemy rail traffic to a virtual standstill after D-Day; and the Cantal area west of the Rhône, where bitter fighting had been in progress since 3 June.

Operation Zebra, the B-17 air-drop by the 3rd Air Division, was originally scheduled for 22 June, but had to be postponed for three days because of bad weather. Finally, at 04.00 hours on 25 June, under clear skies, 180 Flying Fortresses took off from their various airfields in England and set course towards France, being met by the P-47 Thunderbolts and P-51 Mustangs of their fighter escort at various rendezvous points along the route. One bomber was shot down by flak and another by an enemy fighter that slipped through the escort, and two more B-17s had to turn back because of technical trouble. The other 176 went on to drop a total of 2,077 containers on four out of the five designated targets; the Wing assigned to the Cantal drop failed to see any reception, so it diverted to an alternative dropping zone south of Limoges and unloaded its containers there.

At 04.00 hours on 14 July, nine B-17 Wings of the 3rd Air Division took off from nine airfields to carry out their second mass air-drop, Operation Cadillac. The main objective behind this operation was to supply units of the FFI who were fighting hard in support of the Americans at St Lo, preventing large numbers of enemy troops from reinforcing the front. Conscious of this threat to their rear, the Germans were making determined efforts to eliminate the FFI in the Rhône and Saône Valleys, and bitter fighting was in progress to the south-west of Châlons-sur-Saône and in the Limoges area.

The nine Wings of Flying Fortresses were assigned to seven targets in these areas, and were escorted all the way by 521 Mustangs and Thunderbolts. These, however, could not prevent a determined attack by fifteen Messerschmitt Bf 109s south-west of Paris, which crippled two B-17s to such an extent that they had to turn back and make emergency landings on Allied airstrips in Normandy, and damaged one more. The Americans, somewhat optimistically, claimed the destruction of nine 109s, with two probables and three damaged.

Apart from this there was no opposition and the Fortresses flew on to their targets. Two B-17 Wings dropped 860 containers on the Vercors Plateau, while a third Wing dropped 429 containers south-west of Châlons-sur-Saône. The remaining 214 Fortresses dropped 2,491 containers on five objectives in the Limoges area. The operation was highly successful, almost all of the five hundred tons of supplies falling into the hands of the FFI.

On 1 August 1944 the 3rd Air Division carried out another mass drop, five B-17 Wings being assigned to four separate targets. In the Châlons-sur-Saône area, the FFI had used the munitions dropped to them on 14 July to good advantage and had gained control of the Saone et Loire Department; their position was now reinforced by further supplies dropped by a B-17 Wing. A second Fortress Wing dropped 451 containers west of Geneva, and a third dropped 463 containers at a dropping zone in the Alpine region of Savoie, where the FFI had just become reorganized after five thousand of them had fought a savage eight-day battle against German forces earlier in the year. The other two B-17 Wings dropped 899 containers over Haute Savoie. The total number of aircraft involved in this operation was 192, of which six were slightly damaged by flak.

There were no further mass air-drops by the 8th Air Force until 9 September, when seventy-two B-17s flew to a DZ twenty-five miles south of Besançon to drop 810 containers to the FFI. By this time the latter controlled a score of Departments, and as the French linked up with the Allied advance in various sectors the need for air supply diminished.

The Americans, however, were required to undertake one further big air supply operation in September 1944, a month that saw the Polish Home Army fighting desperately to gain control of Warsaw. In the middle of August, in response to desperate appeals from the Polish military authorities, the commander of the US 8th Air Force, General Carl Spaatz, agreed to allocate several groups of B-17s for such an operation, which would have to be carried out in daylight with massive fighter escort and which would depend upon the use of Soviet airfields in the Ukraine.

During the summer months of 1944, under the terms of an agreement already reached with the Soviet Government, US bombers flying from British bases had carried out several shuttle-bombing operations — under the codename of Project Frantic — over Germany, landing at Poltava in the Ukraine. This agreement however had only been reached after months of haggling, and every new flight had to be authorized by the Russians.

The plan was to despatch 110 Flying Fortresses, carrying a total of 1,320 containers. At the beginning of September stockpiles had been built up on three 8th Air Force airfields in England — Horsham, Thorpe Abbots and Tramlington — and the only obstacle to the operation was the attitude of the Soviet Government, who persistently refused to allow the Allies to use their airfields until 12 September, when they finally relented.

118

Whether they did so because continual Allied political pressure was at last having some effect, or because they already knew that the cause of the Polish insurgents in Warsaw was hopeless, is not clear. What is known is that on the night of 13/14 September the Soviet Air Force itself began to carry out supply missions to the Polish capital, and over the next few days it dropped 55 tons of supplies, including 15 tons of food.

The 8th Air Force units earmarked for the operation were immediately placed on readiness, and on 15 September the armada took off. However, the weather was so bad over the North Sea that the aircraft were forced to turn back short of the Danish coast. Fog still persisted in the early morning of the 18th, but the weather forecast for conditions over central Europe were good and the aircraft took off once more.

The 110 B-17s, flying in three tight boxes and escorted by seventy fighters, flew steadily eastwards, stepped up between 13,000 and 16,500 feet. Three of the Fortresses had to turn back with engine trouble; the remainder crossed the Danish peninsula and flew on to the south of the island of Bornholm. Enemy fighters came up to intercept them but the fighter escorts managed to beat off these attacks without too much difficulty. As the Fortresses entered Polish territory, however, the P-51 Mustang fighter escort was forced to turn back at the limit of its range, and now the German fighters were able to press home their attacks unopposed. One of the Fortresses was shot down on the approaches to Warsaw; the remainder pressed on and thundered over the city, dropping their containers into the sea of smoke and flames.

The insurgents watched in disbelief as the multi-coloured parachutes drifted down; many people believed that it was a parachute brigade which was coming to their assistance. In all, 1,284 containers were dropped, of which only 228 fell into the hands of the Home Army. The remainder were widely scattered and most were captured by the Germans. Others were destroyed when their parachutes failed to open.

The Fortresses flew on towards Poltava, losing one more aircraft on the way. A further ten aircraft had suffered such a degree of battle damage that they had to be scrapped. The Fortresses stayed at the Russian base for a week, eventually returning to Britain by way of Italy. By that time the battle for Warsaw was over.[40]

The celebrated 'Pick' – Wing Commander P.C. Pickard, one-time CO of No. 161 Squadron and veteran of many special operations – with his navigator, Flight Lieutenant Alan Broadley. Both were killed in the attack on Amiens Prison in February 1944.

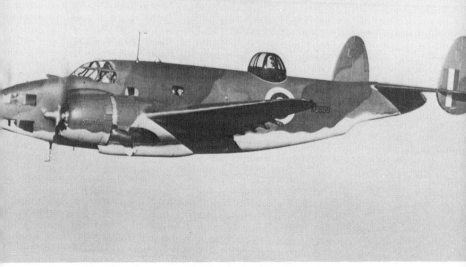

The Lockheed Ventura. Two aircraft of this type were used by No. 1575 Flight and 624 Squadron on clandestine operations in the Mediterranean Theatre.

A Halifax pictured on take-off. This particular example is a B.Mk. I.

Closeup of a Halifax B.III nose. The aerial just above the small window is for 'Rebecca', the radio equipment used to home the aircraft on to 'Eureka' beacons.

PART TWO

Special Duties Air Operations in the
Mediterranean Theatre, 1942-45

8

Clandestine Operations, Mediterranean Theatre: the Royal Air Force

The first Royal Air Force unit specifically created for special duties operations in the Mediterranean Theatre was No. 1575 Flight, which formed at Tempsford on 20 May 1943 with an initial establishment of four Halifaxes and two Lockheed Venturas. On 11 June, two of the Halifaxes left Tempsford for Maison Blanche near Algiers, and these were followed by the other two on the 14th. The Venturas also departed for Maison Blanche on 23 and 24 June.

All these aircraft, with the exception of one Halifax which was unserviceable, left Maison Blanche on 25 June for Blida, in Algeria, which was to be 1575 Flight's operational base for special· duties operations over Corsica, Italy and Sardinia. These operations continued on a limited scale until 22 September 1943, when 1575 Flight disbanded and all personnel and equipment were transferred to the newly-formed No. 624 Squadron.

The Squadron's equipment comprised fourteen Halifaxes, with four more in reserve, and the two Venturas. During the period June-September 1943 No. 624's success record was quite high; out of forty-two sorties to Italy, for example, twenty-nine were successfully completed, but reception techniques at this stage were very faulty and many supplies and agents fell into enemy hands. The period from 1 October to 31 December was less successful, mainly because of adverse weather conditions, and only seven sorties were successfully carried out. In fairness to 624's crews, however, it should be mentioned that the Squadron was often called upon to carry out its secondary bombing role during the closing weeks of 1943.

In January 1944 the Squadron moved to Brindisi, from which

location operations were flown over Yugoslavia and Albania. No. 624 returned to Blida in March and continued operations from there, concentrating now on southern France; the Squadron ORB, in fact, shows little in the way of SD operations to other European objectives during the next three months.

In July 1944 No. 624 Squadron began to re-equip with Stirling aircraft, a change that was not greeted enthusiastically by the aircrews. The Squadron's accident rate immediately took a sharp upward curve, although this appeared in some cases to be the fault of the crews rather than the aircraft, despite the fact that some of the crews recently posted to the unit already had a lot of hours on Stirlings. Of seven accidents that occurred during the first few weeks of Stirling operations, in fact, six were attributable to pilot error, as the Squadron Commander pointed out in a letter dated 25 August 1944 to Headquarters Mediterranean Allied Air Forces.

> I cannot at this moment put my finger exactly on the cause of the trouble, but I intend to however. The captains do not seem to be capable of individual thought or foresight. As an example, I questioned several of them on their probable diversionary airfields; not one of them could answer a single question. They had not thought of looking up any of these airfields either in Squadron Operations or in Flying Control. Before they attempt operations on their own, the pilots, navigators and bomb-aimers are sent out on two and usually three operations with an experienced crew. In addition, they practise night flying, a short night cross-country and day and night dropping practice ... During the past week a programme of ground lectures has been given, and the crews have all been given additional flying practice. It is hoped by this means to stop the rot.
>
> I have no complaints to make on the Stirling aircraft; I consider that it will prove to be a good aircraft for the work on which this Squadron is engaged. It is unfortunate that this series of accidents should happen so soon after its advent in the theatre.[41]

No. 624 Squadron, however, was not to be given much time in which to prove its Stirlings on special duties operations. It

OSLO

TEMPSFORD
LONDON
TANGMERE

BERLIN

WARSAW

PRAGUE

VIENNA
BUDAPEST

PARIS

L.BALATON

BARI
BRINDISI

**SOME STANDARD
LONG-RANGE SPECIAL
DUTIES AIR ROUTES
INTO OCCUPIED EUROPE**

R.McM 82.

disbanded on 24 September 1944, and when it reformed at Grottaglie on 28 December it was for mine-spotting duties in conjunction with the Royal Navy, equipped with Vickers Walrus aircraft.

The second SD squadron in the Mediterranean Theatre was No. 148, which had enjoyed a distinguished bombing career as a Vickers Wellington unit in the Middle East until its disbandment in December 1942. It was reformed in March 1943 at Gambut, Libya, from a unit known as 'X Flight', which — equipped with a small number of Liberators — had been carrying out a limited number of special operations to that date. In April 1943 the Squadron moved to Derna, another Libyan airfield, with an establishment of ten Halifaxes and four Liberators, the latter having belonged to the former 'X Flight', and for the remainder of the year it shared special operations duties in the Mediterranean with No. 624 Squadron.

In January 1944, together with 624 Squadron, No. 148 moved to Brindisi, where both squadrons operated alongside the Polish 1586 Flight. All SD units in the Mediterranean now came under the control of No. 334 Wing, which had been formed the previous November and which had established its HQ at the Italian base.

In March 1944, Squadron Leader Peter Vaughan-Fowler — who had done such valuable work with 161 Squadron — joined No. 148 to command a new Lysander Flight. Designated 'C' Flight, this was formed on 20 March, and Vaughan-Fowler soon found a suitable field at Neverano which could be used to train his pilots in pickup techniques. The first pickup operation by No. 148's Lysanders was mounted on the night of 3/4 May 1944, when two aircraft set out for a location in Greece; unfortunately it ended in failure, one aircraft aborting with engine trouble and the other being forced to turn back when the pilot encountered ten-tenths cloud along his route. However, the operation was carried out successfully on the following night, one Lysander bringing out three passengers and the other four.

In May 1944 'C' Flight began a series of pickup operations from various points in southern France, for which purpose the Lysanders were detached to a forward base at Calvi, in Corsica. The first Lysander operation from this airfield, a 'double', was flown on the night of 4/5 June by Squadron Leader Vaughan-

126

Fowler and Flying Officer N.H. Attenborough, who, after a bumpy and dangerous flight through the Alps, delivered three passengers to a strip east of Lyons, and brought out seven between them. There were no further Lysander flights from Corsica in June, but five operations — three of them doubles — were laid on in July, followed by four singles in August. All of these were flown by Peter Vaughan-Fowler, the last on the night of the 10/11 just a few days before the Allied invasion of the Riviera (Operation Dragoon).

The Lysanders, however, were by no means the only RAF aircraft to undertake pickup operations from Mediterranean bases. On the night of 15/16 April 1944, Dakota FD919 of No. 267 Squadron, a unit based at Bari, was temporarily attached to No. 334 Wing to carry out a dangerous flight to a field near Belzyce, twenty-two miles south-east of Lublin, in Poland. Flown by Flight Lieutenant E.J. Harrod, and with a crew that included a co-pilot drawn from the Polish No. 1586 Flight, the aircraft took off from Brindisi at 20.40 hours on 15 April and touched down at its destination five hours later, after a flight of 800 miles. It spent fifteen minutes on the ground before taking off for Italy with five passengers — including a senior officer of the Polish Home Army — and several hundredweight of valuable intelligence documents on board. The take-off was extremely hazardous, but Harrod coaxed the Dakota into the air and eventually landed at Bari at 05.45 on the 16th.

Another 267 Squadron Dakota flight into Poland took place on 29 May, when Flight Lieutenant O'Donovan landed two passengers in Poland and brought out three, but it was the third trip — on 25 July — that was to prove the most hazardous of all. At 19.40 that evening, Flight Lieutenant S.G. Culliford, a New Zealander, lifted Dakota KG477 into the air from Brindisi and set course for Poland, accompanied by a Liberator of No. 1586 Flight. The latter aircraft was on a separate mission, but its crew had been briefed to accompany the unarmed Dakota on the daylight leg of its flight in case any opposition was encountered. In the event, the outward flight across Yugoslavia was without incident, and as darkness fell the Liberator turned away on its own business.

Apart from some inaccurate flak over Hungary the outward flight was trouble-free, and Culliford brought the Dakota down to land in a cabbage field beside the river Kisielina, several miles to the west of Zabno in southern Poland. Greeted by the reception committee, Culliford learned to his dismay that a German anti-aircraft battery, pulling back from the Russian Front, was billeted less than a mile away in a school building that was also the HQ of a Luftwaffe Police unit. Working quickly, the Poles loaded some thousand pounds of equipment, in sacks and packing cases, on to the aircraft. Culliford did not know it at the time, but it consisted of bits of a V-2 rocket which had exploded over Poland during a test flight; jigsaw pieces that would prove of inestimable value to British Intelligence.

With the gear on board, Culliford opened the throttles to take off, but the ground was soggy and the Dakota's undercarriage became hopelessly bogged. Only after more than an hour of back-breaking effort with spades, bare hands and planks of wood did the aircraft at last come free, but now the pilot discovered that the people detailed to hold the torches that formed the makeshift flarepath had vanished. In fact, they had been ordered to take up defensive positions around the field when it appeared certain that the Dakota would be captured, and some of them had surrounded the nearby school to deal with any Germans who appeared. The latter, however, remained inside; fresh from the misery of the Eastern Front, they had doubtless had enough of fighting. The rest of the story is told in Culliford's report on the operation:

> We ... headed roughly north-west towards a green light on the corner of the airfield. After swinging violently towards a stone wall, I closed my starboard throttle, came round in another circle and set off again in a north-westerly direction. [The Dakota, it should be mentioned, had no brakes; in the struggle to free the machine from the mud, the hydraulic fluid pipes had been severed.]
>
> This time we ploughed along over the soft ground and waffled into the air at 65 mph just over the ditch at the far end of the field. Airborne, we found that we could not raise our undercarriage, having lost all our hydraulic fluid, and finding our speed thus materially reduced, we poured water from the emergency rations into the hydraulic reservoir until we could pump up the undercarriage by hand.
>
> Since we were now fairly late, having spent one hour and

five minutes on the ground, we set course direct for Lagosta Island from the Carpathians. This took us through an area near the Danube known to be infested with night fighters, but we had to get out of Yugoslavia by daylight. We encountered no opposition and came out over Lagosta, though 'George' was unserviceable due to lack of fluid and we had to fly by hand.

Arriving at Brindisi just as the sun was rising, we were — after some deliberation — allowed to land on a runway under construction that was into wind, in view of our brakeless condition. Apart from some slight excitement at the field, everything went very smoothly.[42]

The Dakotas of No. 267 Squadron were to carry out many more pickup operations on behalf of 334 Wing before the end of hostilities. Meanwhile, in June 1944, the special duties squadrons at Brindisi had been hard at work over Yugoslavia, northern Italy and Greece, flying a combined total of 169 sorties, and on 7 June a new RAF Group was formed at Bari in Italy with the object of controlling air support operations on behalf of the partisan forces in the Balkans. This Group, under the command of Air Vice Marshal William Elliott, contained units of no fewer than eight nationalities. No. 334 Wing was absorbed into it, and a little-known fact is that the Group also had two Soviet Air Force units under its operational control, one operating Yak-3 fighters for escort duties and the other Li-2 transports, the Russian version of the Dakota. These were attached to No. 334 Wing after protracted negotiations with the Soviet Government, and were the only Russian units to serve under a Western command during the Second World War. (The author has been unable to establish the designations of these Soviet units; official Soviet Air Force histories make no mention of them, probably for political reasons.)

With 624 Squadron back in North Africa, re-equipping with Stirlings, the brunt of long-range special duties work was borne by 148 Squadron and the Polish Flight. In July the Halifaxes and Liberators were working at full stretch, and during that month No. 148 Squadron lost five aircraft, its heaviest loss since operations began. A sterner test, however, was yet to come.

In the afternoon of 1 August 1944, the Polish Home Army —

urged on by radio broadcasts from the Russians — rose up against the German forces occupying Warsaw, and bitter fighting raged throughout the city. The Poles immediately began to urge their allies, particularly the British, to send the utmost aid to the beleaguered capital with all possible speed. The situation became even more desperate when, as soon as the uprising was under way, the Soviet Army stopped its advance and in some cases withdrew up to six miles, breaking contact with the German forces in the Warsaw sector.

Adverse weather conditions rendered supply-dropping operations over Warsaw impossible for forty-eight hours after the start of the uprising, but on the night of 4/5 August fourteen aircraft — seven from 148 Squadron and the same number from the Polish 1586 Flight — set out from Brindisi for Poland. Of the Polish aircraft, two managed to make successful drops over Warsaw; the remainder failed to do so for a variety of reasons. All returned to base, some with severe battle damage. Of the seven 148 Squadron Halifaxes that set out, one returned early with an unserviceable rear gun turret. On landing, it swung violently and its undercarriage collapsed. The aircraft burst into flames, effectively blocking the runway for a considerable time; fortunately, all the crew escaped. Only one Halifax succeeded in dropping its load to the Warsaw insurgents; one failed to locate its target and four failed to return. The pilots of the missing aircraft were Flight Lieutenant Blynn, Flying Officers McCall and King, and Pilot Officer Crabtree.

This disaster robbed 148 Squadron of both 'A' and 'B' Flight Commanders and left only one officer pilot, Flight Lieutenant R.J.M. Pryor, who assumed temporary command of both Flights. The Squadron's strength was reduced to four serviceable aircraft and one fully effective crew, the latter having only eleven hours to complete before expiry of their tour. The absence of even a nucleus of experienced crews was to have a serious effect on the Squadron's operations during the remainder of August, and a further contributory factor was the slow rate of aircraft replacement.

No. 148 Squadron's next operation was flown on the night of 12/13 August, when seven Halifaxes were detailed for Warsaw. One aircraft cancelled before take-off through technical trouble, and three successfully dropped their loads of supplies. Halifax

EB196 (Warrant Officer Hall) came back short of fuel and the pilot made a successful forced landing near Lecce, with no injury to the crew. Another aircraft, JN958, was so badly damaged by flak that it had to be handed over to No. 144 Maintenance Unit for major repair, depleting the Squadron's effective strength still further. Five Liberators of 1586 Flight also operated over Warsaw on this night, and three of them made successful drops. All the Brindisi-based aircraft had to be diverted to Grottaglie on return, owing to a strong crosswind at base.

Seven Halifaxes of No. 148 Squadron were again detailed for Warsaw on the night of 13/14 August, but of these three failed to take off through mechanical trouble, one returned early and two failed to locate their dropping zones. This night also saw operations over Warsaw by twenty Liberators of No. 205 Group, whose crews were briefed by 148 Squadron's Intelligence Officers; the units involved were No. 178 Squadron from Amendola and Nos. 31 and 34 Squadrons of No. 2 South African Air Force Wing, Foggia.

During the four nights from 13 to 16 August, seventeen Polish and sixty-two British and South African Halifaxes and Liberators attempted to reach Warsaw. Thirty-four of them succeeded, but of this total only twenty were able to make their drops, fifteen of which fell into the hands of the Home Army. These four nights cost the Poles three aircraft, the South Africans seven and the British five — in other words, nearly fifty per cent of those which got through to the Polish capital. A further three aircraft were destroyed when they crashed on landing, and almost all the others were damaged to some degree. No. 148 Squadron's Operations Record tells its own grim and terse story:

14 August. Six aircraft were airborne for special operations on Warsaw. Of these three were successful, two returned early and no news was heard of Halifax JN896 (Pilot Officer Casey). The three successful crews each saw an aircraft shot down over the target, but as no less than eight aircraft went missing from the various squadrons on the same target the evidence is very inconclusive. Halifax JP254 (Pilot Officer Jones) and JN897 (Pilot Officer Johnstone) were damaged by flak, the latter so seriously that it had to be handed over to 144 MU for major repairs.

15 August. Three aircraft were airborne for targets in Poland and one to a target in Italy. Only one aircraft succeeded in dropping on the target in Poland.

16 August. Four aircraft took off for Polish targets. One returned early and two were successful. One aircraft (Pilot Officer D. Tabor) was airborne for an Italian target and was later found to have crashed near Avezzano, everyone on board being killed. Halifax GD319, pilot Flight Sergeant Toft, operating that same night was attacked by an enemy aircraft but managed to break off the engagement and landed safely with the starboard aileron shot away.

18 August. Five aircraft airborne for Polish targets and one for Italy. Three aircraft returned early and the others all failed to drop their loads. A report was later received from the field that conditions were hopeless for dropping in Poland owing to ground haze and fog.

By this time, it was clear that the Allied air forces could never hope to meet the demands of the Polish Home Army, fighting for its life in the streets and sewers of Warsaw. To maintain the insurgents, it would have meant that twenty aircraft would have to get through to Warsaw and deliver their loads successfully each night, a ratio that was completely impossible. Not only was there the weather and the enemy defences to be considered, but many of the crews who were now operating on the long haul to the Polish capital were inexperienced, and even if they managed to reach Warsaw they were often unable to locate the lane leading to the dropping zone through the billowing clouds of smoke that rose up into the night sky. Even Polish crews who knew Warsaw intimately found it almost impossible to pick out landmarks amid the sea of rubble to which their capital had been reduced; only the winding ribbon of the Vistula was a reliable guide. Many lost their lives as they circled in a vain attempt to find a way in; the Germans had set up a ring of sixty 88-mm anti-aircraft guns around the city, in addition to numerous small-calibre weapons such as the deadly 20-mm four-barrelled 'Vierling' cannon. The South Africans, who had been used to daylight bombing operations, suffered particularly badly; in six weeks of operations over Poland Nos. 31 and 34

Squadrons lost twenty-four out of thirty-three Liberators. The desperate situation in Warsaw was summed up by a signal which reached the Polish 1586 Flight from General Sosnkowski, the Polish C-in-C, on 10 August 1944. It read:

> Please convey to our airmen my order as follows: The fate of Warsaw and the Home Army now fighting within its walls depends on a sure and precise drop of arms and ammunition tonight in two places, above all Krasinski Square and Napoleon Square. I realise the great difficulties, but under the present circumstances I demand from our airmen the utmost will-power and self-sacrifice. These two drops must be carried out unconditionally; if necessary the planes should be sacrificed and the airmen bail out. I am sure that the task will be accomplished as my faith in the courage and efficiency of our airmen is boundless.

The Polish crews sensed the urgency and rose to the task as best they could. On the night of 13/14 August a Liberator of 1586 Flight made a drop on Krasinski Square. Several days later, General Sosnkowski sent a signal to Brindisi asking for the name of the captain of the aircraft, to whom he wished to award the Virtuti Militari, Poland's highest decoration for gallantry. He was informed that the pilot, together with his entire crew, had been killed when their aircraft, ablaze from end to end, had crashed on the roofs of the old town seconds after its supply containers had gone down.

During the last two weeks of August no supplies at all got through to the insurgents, although it was not for want of trying. During this period fourteen Allied aircraft were lost, and with the prospect of further serious losses during the September moon period operations to Warsaw were halted.

Meanwhile, on 12 August, Winston Churchill had appealed to the Russians to provide all possible help for the insurgent Poles and also to allow Allied aircraft to land on Soviet airfields. Stalin did not even bother to reply. Two days later a joint request was made by the British and American governments, and in this case the request was met with a flat refusal. Not only did the Russians make it clear that they would not permit the use of their airfields by Allied aircraft engaged in supply operations to Warsaw; they also stated that they would not allow damaged Allied aircraft with wounded on board to land on them. To make the Soviet attitude clearer still, Allied aircrews operating over Warsaw reported that on several occasions they had been attacked and harrassed by Soviet night-fighters.

The Soviet refusal virtually signed Warsaw's death warrant. With the Soviet forces still holding back, only a massive airlift by a strongly-escorted air armada in daylight could possibly redress the situation. The United States 8th Air Force attempted such an operation in September 1944 (see pp. 118-19) but by that time it was too late.

As the Americans prepared their supply operation, the Allied special duties units in the Mediterranean made a last despairing attempt to get through to Warsaw. On the night of 10/11 September, during the eight-day moon period, five Polish, four British and eleven South African aircraft took off from their respective bases in Italy. Seven reached the capital and carried out their drops, but none of the equipment was received by the Home Army, penned now inside an ever-shrinking perimeter. Two more aircraft took off on the following night, but their effort too ended in failure. The last flight was carried out on 21/22 September, and on 2 October the remnants of the Home Army surrendered. It was to be more than three months before Soviet forces finally entered the capital.

Early in October 1944 the special duties squadrons at Brindisi were engaged in air supply operations in support of Operation Manna, the British invasion and occupation of southern Greece. The RAF, in fact, had began sporadic air supply missions to the Greek partisans in 1942 and by the end of 1943 a regular flow of material was being dropped; however, Operation Manna was made possible not because of any large-scale partisan offensive, but because of planned German withdrawals northwards. The RAF effort was supported by C-47s of the USAAF 60th Troop Carrier Group, which also came under the control of 334 Wing, and by the B-24s of the 885th Bombardment Squadron, which made thirty-five sorties to Greek targets in October. During the Greek operations Allied aircraft dropped or landed some 2,700 tons of supplies to the partisans and the British forces, the RAF delivering about two-thirds of the total.

On 7 November 1944, the Polish 1586 Special Duties Flight was officially renumbered No. 301 Squadron, in which guise it continued SD operations — mainly over Yugoslavia — into 1945, when it returned to the United Kingdom and was assigned to ordinary air transport duties. Flying Halifaxes and Vickers-Armstrong Warwicks, it continued in this role until December 1946, when it finally disbanded.

Also in November 1944, No. 148 Squadron received a number of Stirling aircraft, and during operational periods up to the end of the war in Europe these joined the Halifaxes in dropping supplies and agents to targets in Austria, Czechoslovakia, southern Germany and — on a limited scale — northern Italy. The Squadron remained at Brindisi until June 1945, when it moved to Foggia on general transport duties. It later moved to Egypt and disbanded there on 15 January 1946.

The Dakotas of No. 267 Squadron continued in their role of general transport, personnel evacuation and supply dropping to partisans in the Balkan area until February 1945, when the Squadron moved to Burma in support of the 14th Army's final offensive in that theatre. It disbanded on 30 June 1946.

9

*Clandestine Operations, Mediterranean Theatre:
the USAAF*

By the end of January 1944, it was becoming clear that the RAF special duties squadrons of No. 334 Wing would soon have difficulty in meeting the growing demand for air supply to the partisan organizations operating in France, Italy and the Balkans. In February, therefore, the Wing received a welcome boost with the arrival from Sicily of two USAAF units, the 7th and 51st Troop Carrier Squadrons of the 68th Troop Carrier Group, equipped with C-47s.

The Americans lost no time in assuming their new duties. On 7 February, two C-47s carried out Operation Bunghole, which involved the dropping of a team of USAAF meteorologists and their equipment at a drop zone ('DZ') near Ticevo, in Yugoslavia. One missed the target in heavy snow, but the other made a successful drop. This operation was originally scheduled to be flown by the RAF, as was Operation Manhole, the infiltration of a Soviet Military Mission into Yugoslavia, but 334 Wing HQ also assigned this mission to the new arrivals.

The Russians had arrived at Brindisi early in February aboard an Li-2 transport — a Soviet copy of the C-47 — and authority to fly them into Yugoslavia was quickly forthcoming from General Wilson, the Allied C-in-C Mediterranean Theatre. The RAF had planned a daylight landing by Dakota at Medeno Polje, but a heavy fall of snow on the airstrip made this impossible, and so it was decided to use gliders instead. Accordingly, on 23 February 1944 three C-47s of the 51st Troop Carrier Squadron, towing three Waco CG-4A gliders with 23 Russian and 6 British officers on board, took off from Bari and headed for the landing zone ('LZ') escorted by twenty-four P-40

136

A Halifax Mk.V. This variant was used principally by No. 148 Squadron in the Mediterranean Theatre, and by 161 Squadron in the UK. No. 138 Squadron retained the Mk. II.

No photograph exists of a Lysander 'mail snatching' operation, but in this shot a US Army L-19 shows how it was done.

Consolidated B-24 Liberators. This long-range aircraft sustained special duties operations in South-East Asia and was also used by the USAAF on 'Carpetbagger' missions, as well as by some RAF SD units in the Mediterranean.

The North American B-25 Mitchell was the last aircraft to be added to No. 161 Squadron's inventory. One aircraft, modified to drop agents and stores, was supplied for trials just before the end of the war. Had the war continued, the Mitchell would have replaced the Hudson in the SD role.

Kittyhawks of the Desert Air Force and twelve P-47 Thunder-bolts of the US 15th Air Force. The LZ was reached without incident and the gliders made perfect landings, after which the C-47s also dropped supplies.

Unfortunately, very poor weather in February and March 1944 severely restricted supply operations, and of 186 sorties attempted by 334 Wing during this period 62 ended in failure, a further 97 planned operations being cancelled. Most sorties were flown to Yugoslavia, but a few went to Albania, Greece, Bulgaria and southern Italy. Crews also experienced great difficulty in locating reception areas, particularly in Yugoslavia, where partisans were under heavy pressure. On the night of 1/2 March 1944, for example, two C-47s of the 7th Troop Carrier Squadron set out to make a drop at a location seven miles north of Tirane, in Albania. One pilot found the target and flashed his recognition signal, but received an incorrect reply, so he circled the area for an hour and a half waiting for the correct signal before he gave up and returned to base. The other pilot spotted the reception fires, but as he was starting his run-in the fires went out and more were lit some distance away. This happened three times, until the pilot decided that it was prudent to make for home. Later, it turned out that the partisans had been avoiding enemy patrols.

The 7th and 51st Troop Carrier Squadrons returned to Sicily late in March 1944, their place at Brindisi being taken by four C-47 squadrons of the 60th Troop Carrier Group. These carried out their first SD sorties on the night of 27/28 March, dropping leaflets over Italy and the Balkans.

Although pickup operations of up to four agents were undertaken in the main by the Lysander Flight of the RAF's No. 148 Squadron, the 60th Troop Carrier Group quickly specialized in landing techniques at rough airstrips, either to deliver large parties of Allied personnel or to bring out wounded partisans. On the night of 2/3 April 1944, Captains Carl Y. Benson and Floyd L. Turner of the 60th TCG became the first Army Air Force pilots to undertake this kind of operation, landing at Medeno Polje to bring out thirty-six wounded evacuees between them. By the end of the month, the 60th had carried out fifteen C-47 landing sorties to the same airstrip, which was close to Tito's HQ at Drvar, and brought out 168 personnel, including some senior members of the British Military Mission led by the soldier-diplomat Fitzroy Maclean, who was later to immortalize the struggle of the Yugoslav partisans in his book *Eastern Approaches*. The mission had been parachuted into Yugoslavia from a 138 Squadron Halifax in January.[43]

This first C-47 landing mission was so successful that the Americans subsequently sent a party to Medeno Polje to organize proper control facilities and supervise loading procedures. As time went by, more such teams were infiltrated into Yugoslavia and other points in the Balkans, forming what was known as the Balkan Air Terminal Service. Responsible for a wide variety of tasks, BATS personnel organized no fewer than thirty-six landing grounds in Yugoslavia alone during 1944. BATS teams came under the control of the Balkan Air Force, when the latter was formed in June 1944.

On several occasions, the Army Air Force C-47s had to act quickly in response to desperate pleas for assistance from partisans who found themselves surrounded by strong enemy forces. In May 1944, for example, Tito's Headquarters were in grave danger of being overwhelmed by a German offensive; alerted by enemy reconnaissance aircraft, the partisans began to move their HQ from the Drvar area into the comparative safety of the mountains, but the move was incomplete when the Germans launched their attack at dawn on 25 May. While a partisan rearguard fought desperately to hold off the attackers, Tito, his immediate staff and the members of the Allied missions attached to him scattered into the surrounding hills.

While Allied fighter-bombers flew air strikes in support of the partisans, No. 334 Wing carried out emergency supply drops and prepared to evacuate refugees who were encircled in the Prekaja Mountain region. A BATS team was air-dropped to prepare a landing strip in one of the few level places, the Kupresko Valley, and even as Tito's party was assembling the transport aircraft were en route from Italy to airlift them to safety. The first to arrive, on 3 June, was a Russian Li-2 belonging to the squadron attached to 334 Wing; operating out of Bari, it landed in the valley at 22.00, took on Tito and several senior staff officers, flew them safely to Bari and then returned for a second load. Three C-47s of the 60th TCG also flew out seventy-four people that night. Operations continued until the night of 5/6 June, the last C-47 — laden with wounded — taking off only a short time before the airstrip was occupied by the advancing Germans.

During these operations, on the night of 3/4 June, Captain Homer L. Moore of the 28th Troop Carrier Squadron was awarded the Distinguished Flying Cross. Thick cloud had closed over the Kupresko Valley just before he reached the area, but he let down successfully through it, delivered a load of supplies and evacuated twenty-two wounded partisans.

The Germans continued to make determined efforts to destroy the partisans from June to September, launching a particularly strong offensive in Montenegro during July. The partisans took a severe mauling in August and No. 334 Wing operated at maximum effort to keep them supplied; the 60th TCG alone flew 620 tons of supplies into Yugoslavia during this month and made 145 landings, flying out 2,000 refugees. The weather was appalling for most of the time, and the main landing field in use involved a let-down between two jagged mountain peaks, a feat that was miraculously accomplished each time without mishap.

The situation improved during the last week in August and the first week of September, when Romania and Bulgaria capitulated to the advancing Russian armies. This threw the whole German strategic plan into complete chaos, and a desperate scramble ensued as the enemy tried to extricate his forces in reasonable order before the Russians overwhelmed them. The Balkan Air Force, taking full advantage of the sudden reversal of events, flew over 3,500 sorties in September, hammering the Germans' lines of communication, while No. 334 Wing delivered over a thousand tons of supplies to partisans in Yugoslavia and Albania. More than half of this total was carried by the C-47s of the 60th Troop Carrier Group, which made 125 landings in Yugoslavia and brought 1,500 people to safety.

One of the biggest evacuations during this period took place on 22 August, when 900 wounded partisans were moved into an assembly area at Brezna, ten miles north of Niksic. The Yugoslavs cleared some cornfields to make an emergency landing strip, and transport aircraft began a shuttle service that

139

lasted all day. First in were the RAF Dakotas of No. 267 Squadron, which took out 219 wounded; a further 705 were evacuated by 24 Army Air Force C-47s, which also delivered vital supplies, and when darkness fell the Russian Li-2 Squadron attached to 334 Wing airlifted a further 138 partisans to Italy, raising the total to 1,078. Throughout the daylight hours the transports were protected by strong fighter cover.

In September 1944 another USAAF special duties unit arrived in Italy from North Africa. This was the 885th Bombardment Squadron, commanded by Colonel Monro MacCloskey.

Earlier in the year, General Ira Eaker, newly arrived in the Mediterranean from the European Theatre of Operations, had taken steps to initiate regular USAAF special duties operations from North Africa. Some SD flights — mainly involving leaflet dropping — had in fact been carried out on a very limited scale since November 1943 by the 122nd Liaison Squadron, and in January 1944, on Eaker's insistence, this was redesignated the 122nd Heavy Bombardment Squadron and assigned to SD operations as its primary role. Officially formed on 10 April, it was attached to the US 15th Air Force and based at Blida, where it operated alongside No. 624 Squadron, RAF. The activities of both squadrons were co-ordinated by a Special Projects Operations Centre, which selected targets, established contacts in the field, and so on.

The 122nd was fully operational in May 1944, during which month its B-24s completed 45 out of 72 sorties attempted. The official record states that weather and poor navigation caused some of the failures, but the principal cause was the failure to make contact with reception. This improved later in the year when more 'Eureka' sets were supplied to the Maquis.

In June 1944 the 122nd was redesignated the 885th Bombardment Squadron, and shortly afterwards it embarked on a hectic series of operations over southern France in preparation for Operation Dragoon. On the night of 12/13 August, for example — twenty-four hours before the Allied invasion of the Riviera — eleven B-24s operated on targets in southern France, dropping 67,000 pounds of ammunition and supplies, eighteen agents and nearly a quarter of a million leaflets.

In mid-September the 885th moved to Brindisi and came

140

under the operational control of 334 Wing, concentrating its effort now on Italy and the Balkans. The Squadron's first mission to northern Italy had in fact been flown on the night of 9/10 September 1944, from Maison Blanche, and in the two weeks before the move to Brindisi the B-24s undertook thirty-six more trips, dropping fifty-nine tons of supplies to targets in the Po Valley. Nine more sorties were made to the Po Valley during the last week of September, from Brindisi, and during this period the 885th also carried out some escorted daylight sorties to the Balkans.

Before September 1944, northern Italy had been somewhat neglected in the overall scheme of SD operations, but when the Germans launched a major offensive aimed at crushing partisan activity in the Udine area during October operations increased greatly. The 885th Bombardment Squadron attempted eighty-five sorties to targets in northern Italy during the month, but only thirty-three were successful and two B-24s were lost. Bad weather contributed to the failures, but in many cases reception was missing.

The situation improved in November, when the C-47s of the 62nd and 64th Troop Carrier Groups were assigned to Italian supply operations, and in December the 859th Bombardment Squadron also arrived from the United Kingdom. The experience of its crews, by now well used to 'Carpetbagger' operations, was to prove invaluable, and despite continued bad weather sorties remained at a high level throughout the winter of 1944-45. Some sorties to targets in northern Italy were undertaken during this period by aircraft of the RAF's No. 205 Group, but after November 1944 it was the Army Air Force which was responsible for the vast bulk of supplies which reached the Italian partisans.

The C-47s of the 62nd Troop Carrier Group, based at Malignano and Tarquinia, used the former airfield as the starting point for all its operational sorties, which began on 22 November with a mission by six aircraft of the 4th Squadron to a dropping zone near Massa. The C-47s were escorted by two P-47s. The 62nd's other two squadrons, the 8th and 7th, began air supply operations on 28 November and 5 December respectively, the three delivering nearly five hundred tons of supplies by 9 January 1945, when they reverted to normal transport duties. Their special duties task was then taken over on 11 January by the 64th Troop Carrier Group, operating out of Rosignano. The 64th's aircraft completed a thousand sorties by 7 May 1945, dropping 1,800 tons of supplies for the loss of one C-47. Most sorties were flown to DZs in the mountains north-west of Pistoia, but some drops were made in the areas west of Turin.

Meanwhile, the 7th Troop Carrier Squadron had resumed operations to the Balkans from Brindisi in October 1944, followed shortly afterwards by the 51st TCS. The 7th TCS left Brindisi again early in December, but some of the 859th Bombardment Squadron's B-24s were assigned to Balkan targets to make up for this loss. In March 1945 the 16th Troop Carrier Squadron of the 64th Troop Carrier Group replaced the 51st TCS, and continued supply drops to Balkan objectives until the end of the war. At this stage most of the C-47 sorties were going to targets in Albania, the longer-range trips to Yugoslavia being undertaken by the 885th Bombardment Squadron's B-24s; between 18 October and 31 December 1944 this squadron made 256 successful sorties, including one escorted daylight mission by thirteen aircraft to a DZ at Podgorica, in southern Yugoslavia.

The last large-scale evacuation mission undertaken by the Army Air Force's C-47s was Operation Dunn, begun on the night of 25/26 March 1945. Two thousand refugees, in danger of being annihilated by the retreating Germans, were assembled at an area north-east of Fiume. At that time the only Army Air Force unit at Brindisi was the 51st Troop Carrier Squadron, commanded by Major Bruce C. Dunn. The C-47s moved up to a forward base at Zamonico and began a shuttle evacuation immediately; in two days, the twelve aircraft assigned to the operation resuced 2,041 persons and delivered 118 tons of supplies. Many of the refugees were women and orphaned Yugoslav children, and it was a fittingly humanitarian note on which to close a splendid operational record.

PART THREE

Special Duties Air Operations in
South-East Asia, 1942-45

10

Clandestine Air Operations in the
Far East, 1942-45

Following the withdrawal of Commonwealth forces from
Burma early in 1942, it became a matter of great urgency to
obtain accurate intelligence on Japanese movements in
anticipation of the enemy's projected attack on India.
Infiltration of Allied agents into Burma by land was a very
difficult and hazardous operation requiring a nucleus of highly-
experienced jungle trekkers, so in May 1942 the Inter-Services
Liaison Department (ISLD), the Allied intelligence-gathering
organization in South-East Asia, proposed to Air Staff
Headquarters in India that infiltration of agents should be made
by air.* This was approved by the Air Staff, and in June a
Hudson aircraft belonging to the Air Landing School at Delhi
was detached to Dinjan in Assam to carry out the first
clandestine air operation from India. Two agents were dropped
over Burma during the June moon period, and from the RAF
standpoint the operation was a complete success. Because of the
strict security precautions imposed by ISLD there is no official
RAF record of this operation; in fact, throughout the twelve
months during which Air Landing School was involved in this
type of work, no information was kept either at the School or at
Air Headquarters.

*ISLD was independent of SOE, dealing with intelligence gathering while SOE dealt
with field operations, although the two departments worked in close co-operation. In the
Far East, SOE was divided into three zones: Force 136 Group A, which was responsible
for establishing contacts in Thailand and Burma; Group B, which was really a
headquarters group based in Ceylon; and Group C, which covered southern China.
SOE in this theatre of war operated in much the same way as its counterpart in Europe,
the main difference being that its field operatives — Force 136 personnel — usually wore
military uniform and were concerned with sabotage and guerrilla warfare rather than
the gathering of intelligence.

This initial success encouraged ISLD to plan a series of future operations, which were to be carried out during the moon periods of the ensuing months. Unfortunately, the weather conditions and the difficulties of operating single aircraft from advanced landing grounds as far as thirteen hundred miles from base severely handicapped the RAF effort in these early days. Nevertheless, out of the ten sorties attempted between 1 June 1942 and 31 May 1943 six were entirely successful.

These early successes by the crews of the Air Landing School encouraged ISLD to scale up the tempo of air operations. It was soon obvious, however, that the small detachments of Hudsons from the Air Landing School would prove quite inadequate for regular monthly operations, and the fact that the primary role of the school was being adversely affected by the withdrawal of aircraft and crews also had to be considered. Therefore, on 1 June 1943 No. 1576 (Special Duties) Flight was formed at Chaklala, equipped with six Hudson Mk.III aircraft. Its first commanding officer was Squadron Leader J.R. Moore, who had been serving as chief flying instructor with the Air Landing School.

No. 1576 Flight established a forward base at Dum Dum airfield, Calcutta, which brought targets in Burma within range of Hudsons fitted with an extra fuel tank in the bomb bay. However, operations were continually restricted by adverse weather, particularly during the period of the south-west monsoon, and sorties could only be flown during the moon period. There were also considerable navigational difficulties, which were not improved by a shortage of adequate maps. During the first four months after the formation of No. 1576 Flight weather conditions over Burma were particularly bad, and only four operations — two in June and two in August — were attempted during this period. The results were far from spectacular; one agent was dropped in June, followed by a solitary supply container in August. The other two sorties were abortive.

In October 1943 three Hudsons attempted eight operations involving nine sorties, and this time all were successful. However, November was an atrocious month from the weather point of view, and only four operations were attempted out of the twelve requested by ISLD. Two of them were successful.

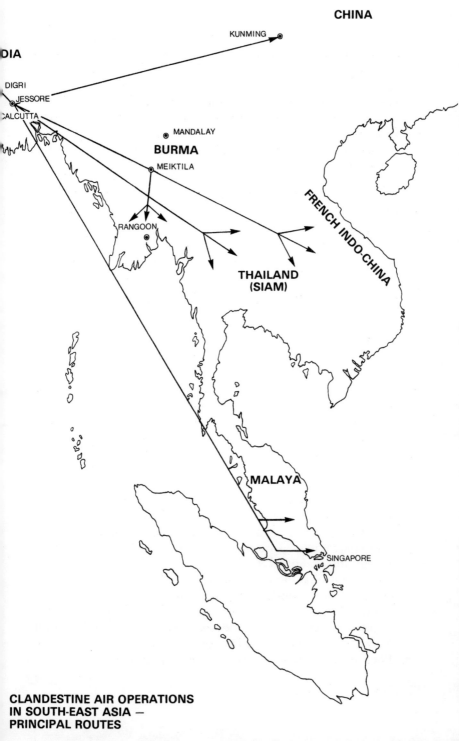

CHINA

KUNMING

DIA

DIGRI
JESSORE
CALCUTTA

MANDALAY

BURMA

MEIKTILA

FRENCH INDO-CHINA

RANGOON

THAILAND (SIAM)

MALAYA

SINGAPORE

**CLANDESTINE AIR OPERATIONS
IN SOUTH-EAST ASIA —
PRINCIPAL ROUTES**

R.MᶜM 82.

To meet the growing need for clandestine air operations outside Burma, three Liberator aircraft were added to the strength of 1576 Flight in November 1943, and it was also agreed that nine Catalina flying boats, shortly due to arrive from West Africa, should be assigned to special duties work. The three Liberators — ex-148 Squadron aircraft — had all been modified to the standard required for special duties operations in the Mediterranean, and further modifications were required before they could be declared operational in their new theatre. One modification involved the replacement of the standard European 'Joe Hole' in the aircraft's fuselage floor by a slide exit.

Six operations were attempted in the December 1943 moon period by 1576 Flight's Hudsons, all of which were successful. No operations were flown in January 1944, however, as weather conditions were appalling. On 1 February 1944, No. 1576 Flight was disbanded and reformed immediately as No. 357 (Special Duties) Squadron, with an establishment of six Liberators, three Hudsons and six Catalinas. 'A' Flight, consisting of the Liberators and Hudsons, was to be based at Digri, while the Catalinas of 'B' Flight were to be stationed at Redhills Lake, Madras. This in itself created problems, because these locations were nine hundred miles apart and the difficulties of operating the two Flights under one command soon became apparent. Air Ministry approval was therefore obtained to form the Catalina Flight into a separate squadron, and this came into being on 21 March 1944 as No. 628 (Special Duties) Squadron.

No. 357 Squadron was not fully installed at Digri until 20 February 1944, and in the meantime its Hudson aircraft continued to operate from Dum Dum during the February moon period, carrying out eight successful sorties on the four available nights. In March, however, special duties operations really began to get into their stride with the delivery of the first six suitably-modified Liberators, enabling 357 Squadron to carry out its first two clandestine operations to Siam. Both were successful, although in one case two attempts were necessary before the operation was completed. In all, during March 1944, twenty-six SD sorties were despatched, of which twenty were successful — the biggest SD effort so far in the South-East Asia Theatre. Unfortunately, this success was marred by the loss of

Hudson AM949 'A', which crashed in mountainous country during a supply-dropping operation at Kokang, on the Burma-China border, killing five of the six crew. This was the first aircraft lost on SD operations in the South-East Asia Command. The surviving crew member, Flying Officer W. Prosser, was eventually brought to safety after a very gallant rescue effort on the part of Flight Lieutenant George Graham, No. 357 Squadron's Medical Officer, who parachuted to the crash site the following morning (16 March 1944) accompanied by Flight Sergeant T.E. White, a parachute jumping instructor with the Air Landing School.

In April 1944 an attempt was made to mount a Liberator SD operation to French Indo-China, using Kunming as an advanced landing ground. This mission, which involved a flight over the notorious 'Hump' of the Himalayas, met with complete disaster. One of the Liberators involved made an emergency landing on a tiny fighter airstrip at Fort Hertz, and the other, after being reported missing, was eventually found to have crashed in northern China, killing all thirteen crew. The tragic failure was attributed to the inexperience of the crews involved. On other operations during April, 357 Squadron Hudsons claimed six successful sorties out of eight, and Liberators five out of six.

During the May moon period the Hudsons completed seven out of twelve sorties, but the Liberators only completed five out of twelve. One Liberator ran out of fuel twenty minutes away from base on the return flight and crashed. The weather during the month was very bad, most crews running into ten-tenths cloud and severe electrical storms. In June the monsoon weather was at its worst, and in the brief periods when operations were feasible the Hudsons flew six sorties. The Liberators, however, managed only one out of nine attempts. Similar weather was experienced during July, the Hudsons completing only three out of nine attempted sorties. The Liberators made two, both of which were successful.

The weather was so bad in August that no operations could be attempted from the home base, but a number of emergency sorties were successfully carried out from advanced landing grounds. In addition, No. 357's Liberators ferried considerable quantities of petrol and lubricants into Kunming for use on future operations. One Liberator sortie was flown from Kunming during the month and another from Sylhet, while the Hudsons completed two out of three attempted sorties from Dinjan, in Assam.

In April 1943, meanwhile, two months before the formation of No. 1576 Flight, special operations by flying boat had also been initiated by ISLD. The first of these was carried out on the night of 22/23 April 1943, when two Catalinas of No. 240 (General Reconnaissance) Squadron, both stripped of non-essential equipment to increase their range, attempted to land agents off the Burmese coast. This first attempt failed, but the operation was completed by the same two aircraft on 25/26 April, one Catalina alighting to disembark the agents while the other dropped hundred pounds bombs on the enemy airfield at Tavoy in order to create a diversion.

The lack of submarine transport for agent infiltration purposes, together with the obvious advantages of air transport, led to a considerable number of Catalina operations being planned by ISLD following this early success. However, general reconnaissance Catalinas were fully committed to their normal duties, and it was not until January 1944 that a second Catalina SD operation was attempted. On 15 January, two Catalinas of No. 240 Squadron set out for an island off the south Burma coast on Operation Buzzard, involving the landing of agents. Once again, one Catalina carried out the actual landing while the other bombed a nearby target as a diversion. The landing was accomplished successfully, although one of the Catalina's perspex observation blisters was smashed and admitted two feet of sea water into the blister compartment. The crew spent nearly three hours of the return flight baling it out. The agents landed in this operation were successfully picked up by No. 240 Squadron Catalina on the night of 14/15 February 1944.

Although formed on 1 February 1944, No. 628 Squadron did not attempt its first special duties operation until May that year, a delay caused mainly by bad weather and poor sea conditions in the selected target areas. On 2/3 May, however, a number of agents and their baggage were put ashore by a 628 Squadron aircraft in the Bangkok area. On 10/11 May, another Catalina went out to make signal contact with this party, but failed to do so. No news was received until ten days later, when an SOS was

150

picked up from the Bassein area; a Catalina landed at a spot on the coast and spent two hours on the water while an ISLD officer went ashore in a vain attempt to locate the fugitive agents. Nothing further was heard from them, and they were presumed to have been captured.

In June 1944, the two RAF special duties squadrons in South-East Asia, Nos. 357 and 628, had fifteen aircraft between them. These aircraft were all old — indeed, the Hudsons of 357 Squadron were obsolescent — and the rigours of operational flying in a tropical climate had led to growing serviceability problems and a constant drain on spare parts. The Hudsons had performed excellent work, but by the summer of 1944 there was an urgent need to replace them with Dakotas for clandestine operations in the narrow, jungle-clad valleys of Burma, where the Squadron's Liberators were not suited. The urgent demands for infiltration and intelligence work in the summer of 1944 were far in excess of the capability of the two under-equipped SD squadrons, and it was clear that there would have to be a substantial increase in the numbers of both short-range supply-dropping aircraft as well as long-range machines.

Accordingly, in September 1944 it was decided to increase No. 357 Squadron's establishment to ten Liberator Mk. VI aircraft and ten Dakotas. This, however, also created a need for an influx of more personnel trained in SD operations, and so the decision was also made to disband No. 628 Squadron and turn its personnel over to the other unit. In any event, No. 628's SD potential had not been fully exploited owing to the difficulty of operating the Catalinas during the months of the south-west monsoon, which had effectively brought flying-boat operations to a standstill.

Also during this phase, considerable effort was devoted to finding a suitable airfield near Calcutta for use as a base for all special air operations and as a centre for packing and stockpiling of SD stores; Digri, No. 357 Squadron's base, was far from suitable because of the lack of adequate road access. Jessore was finally selected as the new operational base, and 357 Squadron moved there in the last week of September 1944.

Despite the administrative problems created by the move, the changeover to new aircraft and the ever-present bad weather, No. 357 Squadron completed twenty-five sorties out of fifty-two

151

attempted during September 1944, while No. 628 — in the last lunar period before its disbandment — made six pickups from enemy waters.

By November 1944 No. 357 Squadron was fully operational with its new complement of Dakotas and Liberators, but the Hudsons remained on strength until January. The last Hudson to fly an SD operation with the Squadron had to be left behind at the Kunming advanced landing ground, unserviceable, after completing a successful pickup from French Indo-China in January 1945. The pilot on this occasion was Flight Lieutenant J. King, who had taken part in the first RAF special duties operation in South-East Asia in June 1942. For his work on SD operations, King was awarded the DSO, DFC and Bar.

Following the disbandment of No. 628 Squadron, two Catalinas and their crews were added to the strength of No. 240 (General Reconnaissance) Squadron at Redhills Lake and earmarked for special duties operations. In the October-November moon period these two aircraft carried out eleven SD operations, of which seven were successful.

During this period, most special duties operations were flown at night, with only a handful of daylight sorties. Nevertheless, during the three moon periods from October 1944 to January 1945, the SD crews completed 95 out of 110 operations, which was quite a remarkable success rate given the prevailing circumstances.

The period from February to May 1945 was one of maximum effort, with the SD crews working hard to put agents into the field and keep them supplied. The official report on SD operations, however, states that the growing efficiency of the Japanese counter-espionage organization, aided by natives who were unfriendly to the Allies, resulted in a harrassing time for the clandestine personnel. Many parties were captured, while others were forced to lie low or keep continually on the move, and reliable native agents were difficult to find. There was some improvement in the situation after the Allied capture of Meiktila, when the Fourteenth Army's advance southwards enabled the clandestine organizations to build up and commit to action considerable friendly guerrilla forces in southern Burma, the main operational areas being the Kerenni Hills and the hill country to the west and south-west of them.

152

In February 1945 the Allies initiated Operation Character, a project to recruit and arm the Kerenni Levies. These were probably the most loyal of all the native populations of Burma, and Force 136 — the Allied force operating behind the enemy lines in South-East Asia in support of guerrilla operations — had been in touch with them since early 1943. The plan was to raise about four thousand Levies to harrass the enemy's lines of communication and retreat in four main areas; north along the Loikaw-Bowlake Road, north central in the Toungoo area, south central in the Kyaukpyi area, and the escape roads to Siam and southwards into the Papun area.

The operation was successful in that it prevented the Japanese 15th Division from taking part in the defence of Toungoo. During the period mid-February to mid-May, special duties aircraft flew 366 sorties to the 'Character' area, dropping 596 tons of supplies to the Levies and native refugees. Japanese casualties amounted to several thousands in the battle but the Levies were sometimes in a very difficult situation; on one occasion, for example, their southern HQ was surrounded for several weeks and relied entirely on air supply. Two hundred Japanese were killed in attempts to take the HQ before its small staff were able to break out.

Early in 1945, special duties aircrews were also involved in Operation Nation, a clandestine operation that entailed the dropping of small groups of Force 136 personnel — usually two officers and a radio operator — at points all over Burma to make contact with the underground movement. The main areas of penetration were Tharrawaddy and Rangoon, and by the time the operations were over the Force 136 agents controlled or were in contact with some seven thousand guerrillas in all areas. In the Toungoo area alone, partisans cut the vital Toungoo-Rangoon rail link twice and killed some seven hundred Japanese.

Special duties aircraft also stepped up operations to China early in 1945, where British military aid groups were operating alongside the Americans and General Chiang Kai-Shek's forces and ISLD coast watchers were monitoring Japanese shipping movements in the South China Sea. Operational difficulties in this area were very great, as clandestine aircraft had to operate out of Kunming and all fuel supplies had to be flown in,

USAAF stocks being very short. A number of RAF SD crews received special training for the long and dangerous flight over the Himalayan 'Hump', but because of the sporadic nature of operations into China they were seldom able to keep in practice. Their task was not made easier by the flying conditions in China, where the weather was — to say the least — unpredictable. Also, RAF pilots suffered from a lack of knowledge of the complicated USAAF system of signals and homing procedures, reasons which might have contributed to the loss of two 357 Squadron Dakotas, one in March and the other in May 1945. Both these aircraft had been carrying medical supplies to British Aid Group parties in China.

Another area of operations to which ISLD and Force 136 paid much attention in the opening months of 1945 was Siam, where the Siamese Army and Air Force were believed to be ripe for open revolt against their Japanese masters. Ostensibly 'co-belligerent' forces, operating alongside Japanese formations, the Royal Thai Armed Forces were in fact nothing of the kind, and a hard core of resistance — particularly among the officers of the Royal Thai Air Force — had grown steadily as the war progressed. The RTAF, luckily, enjoyed a certain amount of freedom from Japanese supervision, and it gradually became the link between the Underground and the Allies. The leader of the resistance movement inside the air force, Colonel Tawi Julasal, had attended the US Naval Academy at Annapolis before the war and was distinctly pro-American, a fact the Japanese appeared to have overlooked.

In 1944-45 agents of both Force 136 and the American OSS were infiltrated into Thailand, some by 240 Squadron Catalinas. On several occasions, OSS agents were flown to Pukio airfield in central Thailand by American C-47 aircraft, where they were met by RTAF pilots, transferred to Thai light aircraft and flown into Bangkok. Another Underground-contact airfield was Noanhan, which was often used as an assembly point for Allied aircrews who had baled out over Thailand.

As a result of this close co-operation between the RTAF and the Allies, British and American attacks on Japanese installations in Thailand were highly effective. For example, Don Muang airfield, the RTAF's principal base, was occupied jointly by the Thais and the Japanese, each using one side of the field. The Thais informed the Allies by radio of the Japanese disposition and the airfield was subjected to a heavy attack by Liberators, which hit only the Japanese-held side. In other cases, Thai units moved out of their permanent bases in deference to the needs of their Japanese 'allies' — having previously ensured that the Americans and British were informed of the changes. The Japanese considered the Thais to be most co-operative, and assumed the fact that the bases were heavily attacked by Allied bombers, within hours of the moves being made, to be purely co-incidental.

Special operations to the other area of vital importance in South-East Asia, Malaya, had presented enormous problems right from the beginning. Although ISLD agents had been operating with guerrilla groups in the Malayan Highlands since 1942, having been infiltrated even before the fall of Singapore, contact since that time had been sporadic, even though several thousand partisans — mainly Chinese — were eventually engaged in active operations against the Japanese. Up to the end of 1944, the main reason for the lack of contact had been a shortage of suitable aircraft to infiltrate Force 136 operatives; submarines had been used on a few occasions to land them in small numbers, but there were few places on the Malayan coastline which were suitable for submarine landing operations.[44]

At the end of 1944, a determined effort was made to begin regular SD air operations to Malaya with No. 357 Squadron's Liberators. This meant taking off at an excessive all-up weight of 66,000 pounds, with only a very small safety margin of fuel. The first such operation was flown in December 1944 and was followed by many record-breaking trips by 357 (and, later, 358) Squadron crews. On one occasion, a Liberator covered a distance of 3,785 miles on a flight lasting 22 hours 55 minutes, and on another an aircraft was airborne for 23 hours 50 minutes. Both these flights departed from Jessore, and the targets were dropping zones less than 100 miles north of Singapore.

The onset of the monsoon in June 1945 made such long-distance flights from Jessore impossible, so during the period up to September the Liberators of 357 Squadron were detached to Minneriya, Ceylon, where they were assisted in their special duties work by the Liberators of Nos. 8 and 160 Squadrons, flying to both Malaya and Sumatra.

Meanwhile, in January 1945, No. 357 Squadron had been joined by another unit specially earmarked for clandestine operations, No. 358 Squadron. This had been formed as a heavy bomber unit at Kolar, southern India, on 8 November 1944 from a nucleus of personnel made available following the disbandment of No. 1673 Heavy Conversion Unit, and, with an establishment of ten Liberators, was under the operational control of HQ 225 Group. On 4 January 1945 it moved to Digri, Bengal, under the control of No. 231 Group and commenced operations nine days later with a bombing attack on Mandalay in central Burma. This was to be its only operation as a heavy bomber unit; immediately afterwards it was assigned to special duties, although it was to revert to a bombing role in the non-moon period each month.

Disaster struck the Squadron very early in its career as an SD unit. On 22/23 January, 1945, three Liberators failed to return from operations over Burma. One aircraft was known to have crashed in the Kalemyo area, but the fate of the other two was never established. The weather was very poor, and it is possible that they went missing somewhere in the Bay of Bengal.

Encounters with Japanese aircraft were infrequent during SD operations, and when they did happen it was usually over Indo-China, although the operations record of No. 358 Squadron tells of one that occurred over Malaya on 21 May 1945, when the crew of Liberator 'T', flown by Flight Sergeant Matthews, sighted three Mitsubishi A6M2-N 'Rufe' floatplanes at 16.05 hours flying north towards Penang, 500 feet above the Liberator which was at 1,500 feet. The Japanese pilots sighted the British aircraft and turned to attack in line astern, whereupon Matthews turned steeply towards the leader. The mid-upper gunner fired a burst of fifty rounds and the leading 'Rufe' sheered off abruptly, followed by the other two. They were not seen again. When approaching the dropping zone at 16.58 hours, Matthews and his crew sighted a 'Thelma' transport flying 200 feet above the target area. The two aircraft passed one another at close range and the Liberator's mid-upper gunner opened fire, reporting that he had seen something fly off the enemy aircraft, which did not alter course and flew on until it was lost to sight.

Thirty minutes after making the drop, Flight Sergeant Matthews spotted another 'Rufe', flying 200 feet below the Liberator on a reciprocal course. The enemy aircraft turned and followed the Liberator until the latter entered cloud, when contact was lost.

The next encounter came at 09.30 hours on 23 May, when the same pilot and crew sighted eight Nakajima Ki.43 Hayabusa ('Oscar') fighters 100 miles north-east of Rangoon near the Salween River, while the Liberator was running-in towards its dropping zone. Matthews briefly lost sight of the enemy aircraft behind a cloud, but they reappeared shortly afterwards, five aircraft closing in from the port side and three from the starboard, adopting a stepped-up attack formation as they did so. Faced with such odds, Matthews lost no time in diving into a sheltering cumulus cloud and managed to break contact with the enemy. He could have got below the cloud and carried out his drop, but reasoned that if the Oscars followed him he risked not only being shot down but also compromising the DZ, so he abandoned the sortie and returned to base.

A far more disastrous encounter with the enemy occurred on 29 May, when Liberator EW174 'P', flown by Flying Officer H.V. Smith RCAF, a Canadian from Winnipeg, was attacked by nine 'Oscars' while on operations over Thailand. The Japanese fighters made a series of accurate head-on attacks, killing the second pilot, Flight Sergeant Poole, the navigator, Flight Sergeant Brenchley and the mid-upper gunner, Sergeant Pinkney. All four engines were quickly put out of action and the Liberator began to lose height rapidly. With great skill, Smith brought the aircraft down for a crash-landing in the jungle. The treetops cushioned some of the impact, but the Liberator broke up as it fell. Nevertheless, six of the crew and three of the four passengers — all American OSS officers — escaped from the wreckage alive, two others being killed in the landing. These were the bomb-aimer, Flight Sergeant Draper, and a US Army NCO, Corporal Naparolski. All the survivors were badly injured with the exception of the rear gunner, Flight Sergeant Copley, who sustained only cuts and a sprained back.

With the help of friendly Thais, Copley and Smith eventually reached Bangkok, where they were hidden until they were flown to a remote Thai airstrip in light aircraft of the RTAF. From there they were picked up by a Dakota of No. 357 Squadron, and returned home less than three weeks after they had been shot down. The other survivors, after being interned by the Thais while they recovered from their injuries, were also flown out by Dakota about two months later.[45]

Fortunately, combats with Japanese fighters were extremely rare. Throughout long-range special duties operations in South-East Asia, it was the weather that remained the main enemy.

No. 357 Squadron Lysander Flight Operations, 1945
Following the disbandment of No. 161 Squadron's Lysander Flight in October 1944, three of the Squadron's experienced pilots — Flight Lieutenant George Turner, Flight Lieutenant Peter Arkell and Flight Lieutenant J.E.M. Williams — were posted to India in December to form the nucleus of a Lysander pickup flight in No. 357 Squadron. Their aircraft, all ex-161 Squadron machines, were to follow by sea after a thorough overhaul. The three Lysander pilots arrived at Jessore by air from Santa Cruz to a thoroughly warm welcome, for No. 357 Squadron's commanding officer at this time was none other than Wing Commander L.M. 'Bob' Hodges, DSO, DFC, back at the sharp end of special duties work after his spell at the RAF Staff College.[46]

In addition to the Liberators and Dakotas, No. 357 Squadron now had a 'C' Flight composed of a miscellany of light aircraft — Harvards, Austers and Stinson L-5 Sentinels — which were used on communications duties with No. 231 Group. Flight Lieutenant Turner took over command of 'C' Flight on his arrival, and the three newcomers quickly familiarized themselves with the L-5 and Auster aircraft. Peter Arkell left on L-5 detachment to RAF Cox's Bazaar, where he carried out Army liaison work, while Turner and Williams remained at Jessore and carried out routine communications flights to Alipore for the time being.

In January 1945 a fourth pilot, Flying Officer Varanand, was posted to 357 Squadron 'C' Flight after a fighter tour in Normandy. His posting was essentially political, for he was a prince of the Thai royal household, and it was felt that his presence in the pickup flight would have enormous propaganda value if pickup operations were extended to Thailand. (They were not, and as far as can be ascertained from the ORB this pilot never flew on clandestine operations.)

On 3 February 1945 Flight Lieutenant Williams went on L-5 detachment to Akyab and Ramree, leaving Turner at Jessore to carry out routine mail runs. When he was not flying, Turner spent a good deal of time in conference with Force 136 HQ at Jessore, drawing up a plan for future pickup operations. As far as training was concerned Bengal had little to offer, for 95 per cent of the countryside was under cultivation and divided into paddy fields, but a suitable area was eventually found only eight miles north of Jessore; it was a group of fields with a hard surface, covered with closely-cropped grass.

In mid-February, 357 Squadron received a signal to say that ten Lysanders had arrived in crates and were being assembled at No. 320 MU, RAF Karachi; the first five would be ready for delivery by 1 March and the other five a month later. All the Lysander pilots were to go to Karachi to ferry the first five aircraft back to Jessore. Some reorganization of 'C' Flight was necessary to make room for the new aircraft, so all the L-5s were transferred to No. 231 Group Communications Flight at Alipore.

The first Lysander to arrive at Jessore, on 3 March, was V9818; unfortunately its stay was short-lived, because it crash-landed on arrival and had to make an ignominious return to Karachi by road for repair. The second aircraft, V9494, flew in on 6 March, and by 26 April 'C' Flight had nine Lysanders, the majority flown to Jessore by ferry pilots. These included V9818, which had been repaired at Jodhpur, but it arrived minus its long-range fuel tank, which had been damaged beyond repair.

On 29 April 1945, on completion of suitable pilot training, a Lysander detachment was sent to Meiktila; this consisted of seven aircraft, and they became an operational flight the following day under the control of No. 221 Group, although for operational purposes the aircraft were under the orders of Force 136 Tactical HQ. The first operation was carried out on 3 May, when Peter Arkell flew to Mewaing with ammunition and supplies and brought out two wounded partisans, one of whom was a woman. He reported that the landing strip was excellent.

On 6 May, Arkell and George Turner flew a double Lysander operation to Mingaladon, in the Rangoon area, to infiltrate four

Force 136 officers. The Lysanders were among the first Allied aircraft to land at Mingaladon after the Japanese evacuation of Rangoon and the pilots found that the airstrip was far from serviceable, having been heavily bombed. Nevertheless, the Lysanders were able to touch down safely on the sole remaining stretch of intact runway. That evening, three of the Flight's Lysanders, T1688, V9295 and V9649, were destroyed by a freak gale-force wind that swept over Meiktila. The Flight's aircraft strength never fully recovered from this disaster.

On 13 May, Flight Lieutenant Arkell completed the highest-ever Lysander pickup so far, landing his aircraft at a strip 5,000 feet above sea level at Hwariku in Burma's Shan State to evacuate a seriously wounded casualty. The landing and take-off were both tricky, because the strip was boggy. On 16 May, George Turner, newly promoted to Squadron Leader, damaged his Lysander in an attempt to pick up personnel at Ngapyawdaw, near Kinmun, and soon afterwards the strip came under threat of attack by Japanese forces. The aircraft could not be repaired on the spot and, partly due to enemy action in the area and partly to the weather, no rescue attempt could be made until 26 May, when four L-5s flew in to take out Turner and several Force 136 officers. During his enforced stay in Burma Turner was entertained at the local Force 136 Headquarters, code-named Mongoose Blue, and made a long daily trek to the airstrip along jungle paths in the hope that help would arrive.

One more pickup operation was flown before the end of May, when a Lysander (pilot unknown) landed at Lipyekhi in the Karen Hills at an altitude of 2,800 feet. The ORB records that when the monsoon began this strip became unserviceable, but another was found nearby on the side of a mountain slope. The strip was the most hazardous of all those used by the Lysanders, but landings were made there constantly throughout the monsoon period.

These early Lysander sorties into Burma were literally ventures into the unknown, as none of the pilots had any experience of the terrain or of mountain flying. The targets were obscure strips on mountain slopes, tiny jungle clearings or patches of paddy, surrounded by hills and for most of the time shrouded in cloud and rain. They could only be reached by very accurate and continual map-reading; with no navigational aids except a compass and a 1:500,000 map the pilots had to fly in visual contact with the ground all the time, which meant that during the peak months of the monsoon — which also happened to be the peak operational period — the pilots were forced to fly very low to keep beneath the cloud base, following the lines of rivers and threading their way through mountain passes. It was hardly surprising that the pilots rapidly gained an intimate knowledge of the topography and weather characteristics of their operational area, and with it a wealth of experience in the tricky technique of mountain flying.

On 26 May, the Lysander Flight moved to Mingaladon, Rangoon, and henceforth operated from there. The first sortie from the new location was made on 3 June, when Flight Sergeant Castledine, a relative newcomer to the Flight, landed at Lipyekhi with supplies for Force 136 guerrillas. To his dismay he found that the airstrip was under fire, and to make matters worse the engine refused to start for the return flight to Mingaladon. Firing continued across the strip all day, but the Lysander miraculously escaped damage and was made serviceable the following morning by a mechanic who flew in aboard a rescue aircraft.

Sorties continued at a rapid rate, some involving pickups and others 'free drops' of supplies to Force 136 groups. The maximum load that could be carried by the Lysander on free dropping operations was 420 pounds, excluding a crew member acting as despatcher in the rear cockpit, and the stores were dropped in padded sacks, which weighed 80 pounds on average. The procedure was to make an initial circuit of the target at 100 mph with the rear cockpit hood fully opened and the despatcher ready to drop; the approach to the target was then made at 75-80 mph, with engine controls and aircraft trim set as for landing and the drop being made at the lowest safe height, which was governed by obstacles in the vicinity. The height, consequently, varied from ten to a hundred feet. The packages were dropped over the port side of the fuselage, the pilot taking care to maintain the correct speed so that they cleared the tailplane. On the over-shoot, the rear cockpit hood was closed to facilitate the rate of climb, the despatcher opening it again on the next circuit. An average of five runs were made, into wind whenever possible.

Notable sorties during June 1945 included the evacuation of wounded Japanese nurses, captured during a Force 136 attack, from a strip at Kyeingon by two Lysanders on the 4th, and the flying out of thirteen passengers, including Japanese prisoners, by four Lysanders on the 16th. The ORB notes that the Lysander Flight completed its fiftieth operational sortie on 18 June.

On 21 June, a Lysander attempted a landing on a very short, wet and slippery grass strip at Htilawthihta near the Papun-Kamamaung road. The aircraft slid into a wide ditch at the far end of the strip but escaped with only light damage. A team of elephants was brought to extricate it but the animals would not go near the aircraft despite determined coaxing, so in the end it had to be pulled out by fifty villagers. The aircraft flew safely back to base, and after this episode that particular strip was abandoned. An appropriate comment on the state of some of the strips used by the Lysanders was delivered by one Captain Fielding, an American war correspondent who was flown into Force 136 'Hyena' HQ on 22 June; he stepped from the aircraft, took one look at his surroundings and the patch of grass on which the Lysander was sitting, and muttered: 'Good God!'

On 27 June, a Lysander flown by Flight Sergeant Castledine became bogged on the strip at Mewaing, and the pilot showed considerable initiative in laying down an improvised runway of bamboo strips from which he was able to take off the next day. This strip was subsequently enlarged and drainage channels dug, and it became one of only three strips that remained usable throughout the June-July monsoon.

The Lysander Flight flew fifty sorties in June 1945 with four available aircraft, and this high sortie rate was maintained during the first part of July. Because of the unserviceability of the various airstrips, many of the sorties involved free drops. By 11 July the total sorties flown had risen to 100; the Flight now had six aircraft, and steady replacements maintained this average for the duration of operations. Sometimes, Lysanders had narrow escapes when the strips they were heading for were found to be compromised by Japanese forces; on 19 July, for example, two aircraft preparing to land at Lipyekhi were warned away by red Very lights because a battle was taking place below.

On 3 August, the Lysanders began a four-day series of ammunition drops which effectively enabled Force 136 troops to prevent a determined Japanese effort to cross to the east bank of the Shwegyin Chaung. Leaflets were also dropped on the Japanese by a Lysander on 4 August, timed to coincide with Allied fighter strikes. On 6 August, another Lysander flew a Flying Officer Snelling, who was a Japanese interpreter, to the strip at Mewaing; from there he travelled to the Shwegyin by elephant and spent some time shouting surrender terms across the river to the enemy.

After 15 August, the date of the Japanese surrender, the Lysanders were employed in dropping surrender leaflets and instructions to Force 136 personnel at DZs throughout the Karen Hill range for distribution among the enemy. During these operations, on 24 August, Flight Lieutenant Peter Arkell crashed near the landing strip at Lipyekhi while attempting to make height on an overshoot; he suffered shock and a compound fracture of the left arm, and was airlifted to safety by a Lysander the following day.

On 30 August, two Lysanders became the first single-engined Allied aircraft to land at Domaung Airfield, Bangkok, after the Japanese surrender, the first landings having been made by Dakotas of 357 Squadron two days earlier. The Lysanders flew out some British PoWs and made two more sorties to Bangkok on the same errand during the next couple of days. On 3 September, the Lysander Flight received news that a Dakota carrying a load of PoWs had crashed some miles inland from Moulmein and that the RAF crew and passengers were awaiting evacuation from a sandy beach to the south of the crash site. Unfortunately, the first Lysander that tried to land on the 450-yard strip of beach crashed into some rocks and was written off, although the pilot escaped with cuts and bruises. Other Lysanders succeeded in landing safely, and in eight sorties on 4 and 5 September they took off thirty-two personnel including the Lysander pilot, Flight Sergeant Stubbings.

During September, the Lysanders were used to reconnoitre former Japanese airstrips in Burma, and in some cases became the first Allied aircraft to land on them. On 10 September, three Lysanders landed at Tavoy with a load of Army officers, who set about the peaceful liberation of the local internment camp, and the aircraft flew out eight internees who were in urgent need of medical attention. Another task in September was to land Japanese Army Officers in the Kerenni Hills; in all, twenty-one Japanese Army personnel were landed at various strips throughout the month, with the object of contacting stray Japanese forces and organizing their surrender.

In October, with the passing of the monsoon, many new strips were opened to facilitate transfer of personnel between the various sectors in Burma, and during this month the Lysanders were employed on communications work of this kind. On 4 November the Lysander Flight completed its 400th sortie, and on 7 November — the date on which No. 357 Squadron disbanded — it was attached to AHQ Burma Communications Squadron, where it was to remain for the rest of its short career.

Notes

1. *The Aeroplane*, 13 October 1915 — report from a Danish correspondent.
2. R. Navarre: 'Mes Aventures guerrières et autres', *La Vie Aérienne*, 14 August 1919, p.525.
3. X. Mortane, *Special Missions of the Air*, London, 1919 (trans).
4. Ibid.
5. 'Flight Commander', *Cavalry of the Air*, London, 1918, p.180.
6. Captain Wedgwood Benn, *In the Side Shows*, London, 1919; G.A. Drew, *Canada's Fighting Airmen*, 1930.
7. C.H.A. Andre, *Au-dessus des Batailles*, Paris, 1917.
8. Colonel A.J.L. Scott, *History of Sixty Squadron, RAF*, London, 1920.
9. René Fonck, *Mes Combats*, Paris, 1920.
10. X. Mortane, *Special Missions of the Air*.
11. P. Bewsher, *Green Balls*, London, 1919.
12. Lt-Col. T.W. White, *Guests of the Unspeakable*, London, 1928.
13. Capt. H. Birch Reynardson, *Mesopotamia, 1914-15*, London, 1919.
14. Lt-Col. J.E. Tennant, *In the Clouds Above Baghdad*, London, 1920.
15. H. Neumann, *Die deutschen Luftstreitkrafte im Weltkriege*, Berlin, 1920.
16. Lt. Emrich, 'Ma Mission Spéciale', *La Guerre aérienne*, 19 December 1918.
17. P.A. Rockwell, 'Les Americains à la Legion', *La Guerre aérienne*, 19 July 1917.

18. Wng Cdr H.A. Jones, *Over the Balkans and South Russia*, London, 1923.
19. M.R.D. Foot, *History of the Second World War - SOE in France*, London, 1966.
20. For a graphic account of Nesbitt-Dufort's pickup operations and adventures in France, see his book *Black Lysander* (Jarrolds, London, 1973).
21. A full account of this operation appears in No. 138 Squadron ORB.
22. Report by Murphy and Nesbitt-Dufort in No. 161 Squadron Operations Record Book (Public Record Office, Ref. AIR 27/1068).
23. See Foot, *SOE in France*, p.67.
24. Hugh Verity's book *We Landed by Moonlight* (Ian Allan Ltd, 1978) is probably the best personalized account of 161 Squadron pickup operations ever published. As well as giving full details of Lysander operations from Tempsford, it also provides intriguing personal glimpses of the characters of the pilots and agents involved.
25. No. 138 Squadron Operations Record Book.
26. Foot, *SOE in France*, Appendix C.
27. Frank Griffiths, *Winged Hours* (Kimber, 1981).
28. No. 161 Squadron ORB.
29. For a full account of this fascinating and highly secret operation, see David Irving, *The Virus House* (Kimber, 1967).
30. Peter Churchill, *Duel of Wits* (Hodder, 1957).
31. It should be pointed out that the Halifaxes usually carried out three or more drops in a single sortie at different locations; if all these objectives were attained the sortie was deemed to have been a complete success.
32. See Bruce Marshall, *The White Rabbit* (Evans, 1952).
33. Verity, *We Landed by Moonlight*.
34. Between this date and the end of the war, several other RAF squadrons — both transport and main force bomber units — were called upon to undertake special operations from time to time. Squadrons known to have been involved were, in numerical sequence, Nos. 75 (Stirling), 90 (Stirling), 149 (Stirling), 196 (Stirling), 199 (Stirling), 214 (Stirling), 295 (Albemarle), 299 (Stirling), 570

(Albemarle), 620 (Stirling), and 622 (Stirling). Special operations by these squadrons involved the dropping of supplies to resistance forces rather than the dispatch of agents.

35. Frank Griffiths, *Winged Hours*.
36. For a full account of Dericourt's controversial activities, see Foot, *SOE in France*.
37. No. 161 Squadron ORB and G. McCall, *Flight Most Secret* (Kimber, 1981).
38. For a popular account of the SOE career of this heroic woman, who was eventually captured by the Germans and executed at Ravensbruck, see R.J. Minney, *Carve Her Name with Pride* (Newnes, 1956).
39. Mahurin also destroyed 3½ MiG-15s over Korea, where he commanded the 4th Fighter Intercepter Group (F-86 Sabres) until being shot down and captured by the communists on 13 May 1952.
40. Excellent accounts of the USAAF's special duties operations are to be found in Craven and Cate, *The Army Air Forces in World War II*, vol. III, and M. MacCloskey, *Secret Air Missions* (Richards Rosen Press, New York, 1966). Brigadier General Monro MacCloskey commanded the 885th Bombardment Squadron (SD) in 1944.
41. Report attached to No. 624 Squadron ORB.
42. No. 267 Squadron ORB.
43. Fitzroy Maclean, *Eastern Approaches* (Jonathan Cape, 1951).
44. For a very comprehensive account of SOE operations in Malaya, see Ian Trenowden, *Operations Most Secret* (Kimber, 1978).
45. For a full account of Copley's and Smith's adventures, see Robert Jackson, *When Freedom Calls* (Arthur Barker, 1973).
46. Known universally as 'Bob', Wing Commander L.M. Hodges remained in the RAF after the war, eventually retiring as Air Chief Marshal Sir Lewis Hodges, KCB, CBE, DSO, DFC.

No. 138 Squadron
No. 138 Squadron was originally formed on 1 May 1918, but
was held in reserve, its aircraft and personnel providing
reinforcements as needed for operational units. Formation was
suspended on 4 July 1918. The Squadron was eventually
reformed on 30 September 1918 as a fighter reconnaissance unit
at Chingford, in Essex, but it never became operational and was
disbanded on 1 February 1919.

On 25 August 1941, No. 138 Squadron was reformed from
No. 1419 Flight at Newmarket, and throughout almost the
whole of the war its task remained the air supply of resistance
movements in occupied Europe. It was originally equipped with
Whitleys and Lysanders, but the latter were taken over by 161
Squadron early in 1942 and Halifaxes began to replace the
Whitleys in October that year, by which time the Squadron was
·operating from Tempsford. Stirlings replaced the Halifaxes in
September 1944. On 9 March 1945 No. 138 reverted to main
force bombing duties and re-equipped with Lancasters.

In September 1947 it converted to Avro Lincoln bombers,
which it operated until its disbandment on 1 September 1950.
On 1 January 1955 it reformed again at Gaydon, in
Warwickshire, and became the first squadron to equip with
Valiant jet bombers. It used these aircraft in attacks on
Egyptian targets during the Suez Crisis of 1956, operating from
Malta, and remained as part of the RAF's V-Force until its final
disbandment on 1 April 1962.

No. 148 Squadron

No. 148 Squadron began its career as a night bomber unit at Andover on 10 February 1918, equipped with F.E.2b and 2d aircraft, and went to France in April, just in time to help counter the last great enemy offensive of the war. From April to November 1918, still flying F.E.s, it took part in many raids on German bases and communications behind the lines. It returned to England in February 1919 and disbanded on 30 June that year.

No. 148 reformed at Scampton on 7 June 1937 from a detachment of No. 9 Squadron and, after a short spell operating Hawker Audaxes, equipped with Vickers Wellesley bombers. These were replaced by Handley-Page Heyfords in November 1938, and these in turn gave way to Vickers Wellingtons in March 1939. From April 1939 until April 1940, No. 148 also operated eight Avro Ansons and was responsible for training bomber crews for No. 6 Group. On the outbreak of war in September 1939 it moved to Harwell and was redesignated No. 15 Operational Training Unit. It reformed briefly as a Wellington squadron at Stradishall on 30 April 1940, but disbanded on 23 May.

On 14 December 1940 it again reformed with Wellingtons, this time at Luqa, Malta, from detachments of Nos. 38, 99 and 115 Squadrons, and until March 1941, when it moved to Egypt, it was heavily involved in attacks on enemy targets in Sicily, Italy and Libya. It continued to operate from Kabrit and various desert landing strips against the Axis supply lines in North Africa until disbanded yet again on 14 December 1942.

On 14 March 1943 it reformed from a unit at Gambut known as 'X' flight, which — equipped with four Liberators — had been carrying out special operations on a limited scale. With a mixed complement of Liberators and Halifaxes, No. 148 began special duties flights to the Balkans, which would be its main area of operations. Halifaxes had completely replaced the Liberators by early 1944, when a Lysander Flight was added for pickup operations. Now based at Brindisi, in Italy, the Squadron devoted much attention to long-range operations to Poland during 1944, and suffered considerable losses at the time of the Warsaw Uprising. In the closing months of the war it extended its area of operations to northern Italy, Austria and southern Germany. In June 1945 it moved to Foggia for general transport duties, then returned to Egypt to be disbanded on 15 January 1946.

In November 1946 it reformed at Upwood with Avro Lancasters, converting to Lincolns in January 1950. Disbanded again on 1 July 1955, it reformed at Marham on 1 July the following year as a V-Force squadron with Valiants, which it took to Malta in October for attacks on Egyptian airfields. The Squadron's final disbandment came in April 1965, when the Valiant was withdrawn from service.

No. 161 Squadron

Originally formed on 1 June 1918 as a day bomber squadron, No. 161 existed for less than a month before being disbanded, its personnel being allocated to other units as replacements.

On 15 February 1942, it reformed at Newmarket with personnel and aircraft drawn from No. 138 Squadron and the King's Flight and began special operations immediately, using Lysanders — later joined by Hudsons — for pickup operations and Whitleys for long-range parachute missions. From November 1942 Halifaxes began to replace the Whitleys, and these remained the standard long-range type until September 1944, when the Squadron received Stirlings. With these aircraft the Squadron continued its supply-dropping operations until the end of the war in Europe, eventually disbanding on 2 June 1945.

No. 240 Squadron

No. 240 Squadron was formed at Calshot in August 1918 from personnel and equipment drawn from Nos. 345, 346 and 410 Flights, which operated a mixture of F.2a flying boats and Short seaplanes. It carried out anti-submarine patrols over the English Channel until the end of the war, and disbanded on 15 May 1919.

Reformed at Calshot on 30 March 1937 and equipped with Short Scapa flying boats, its role was operational training until January 1939, when it was re-equipped with Short Singapores and SARO Londons in quick succession. The outbreak of war in September 1939 found it at Invergordon, and its aircraft patrolled the North Sea until May 1940, when it moved to

Pembroke Dock to patrol the Western Approaches with Stranraers. In July it went to Oban, where it began to re-equip with Catalinas in March 1941 before moving to Lough Erne in Northern Ireland for patrols over the Atlantic.

In June 1942 it moved to India, where it began patrols over the Bay of Bengal and the Indian Ocean from Redhills Lake. It was assigned to special operations in April 1943, landing agents off the Burmese coast, but it was not until early in 1944 that the next Catalina SD operations were attempted. It continued to fly sporadic SD missions to Burma, Malaya and the Dutch East Indies until 1 July 1945, when it was disbanded, but it was reformed that same day by the renumbering of No. 212 Squadron, which was then converting from Catalinas to Sunderlands. Up to the end of the war its main role was meteorological survey; in January 1946 it moved to Ceylon, where it disbanded on 31 March.

On 1 May 1952, No. 240 Squadron reformed at St Eval, Cornwall, with Avro Shackleton maritime reconnaissance aircraft. In June 1952 it moved to Ballykelly, Northern Ireland, where it was renumbered 203 Squadron on 1 November 1958.

No. 240 Squadron had a further brief lease of life between 1 August 1959 and 8 January 1963, when it operated as a Thor strategic missile squadron at Breighton until its disbandment.

No. 267 Squadron

Formed at Kalfrana, Malta, in September 1918 as a flying boat unit, No. 267 Squadron flew anti-submarine patrols until the end of the war and remained operational until 1 August 1923, when it disbanded. It reformed at Heliopolis, Egypt, on 19 August 1940, and for the next eighteen months carried mail and freight between Egypt and other bases in the Middle East, using a miscellany of aircraft types. Apart from light aircraft such as the Percival Proctor and Gull 6, these included Hudsons, Wellesleys and Lockheed 14s.

In the summer of 1942 No. 267 Squadron received its first Dakotas, and these were to become standard equipment for the remainder of the war. In November 1943 the Squadron moved to Bari, Italy, and undertook many special duties operations to the Balkans, dropping supplies to resistance workers and evacuating partisans. This work continued until February 1945,

171

when the Squadron moved to Burma in support of the 14th Army offensive that finally drove the Japanese from that country. At the war's end, No. 267 carried out general transport duties until its disbandment on 30 June 1946.

No. 267 reformed on 15 February 1954 at Kuala Lumpur, Malaya, as a support and communications unit, operating a mixture of Pioneers, Pembrokes and Dakotas. It was renumbered 209 Squadron on 1 November 1958, but reformed as 267 Squadron on 1 November 1962 as a No. 38 Group transport squadron, operating Armstrong Whitworth Argosies from Benson, Oxfordshire. It disbanded on 30 June 1970.

No. 357 Squadron
No. 357 Squadron formed at Digri, India, on 1 February 1944 from No. 1576 (Special Duties) Flight, with an establishment of seven Hudson VIs, three Liberator IIIs and, briefly, four Catalinas, the latter based at Redhills Lake. The Squadron's Hudsons and Liberators carried out many agent- and supply-dropping flights over Burma, Thailand, Indo-China and China, the Liberators flying almost as far as Singapore at the limit of their range. By the end of 1944 the Hudsons had been replaced by Dakotas, and early in 1945 a Lysander Flight was added to the Squadron's strength for pickup operations in Burma. At the end of hostilities the Lysanders were engaged on communications work, and 357 Squadron disbanded on 15 November 1945.

No. 358 Squadron
No. 358 Squadron was formed at Kolar, India, as a heavy bomber unit from personnel of No. 1673 Heavy Construction Unit, which had recently disbanded. Its initial complement was sixteen Liberators. The Squadron carried out its first (and only) bombing mission from its new base at Digri on 1 January 1945, when eight aircraft attacked Mandalay. After that it was assigned to special duties work, completing many long and hazardous sorties to dropping zones all over South-East Asia before hostilities ended, when its Liberators were used to drop supplies to PoW camps in Malaya, Java and Sumatra. The Squadron disbanded on 21 November 1945.

No. 624 Squadron

No. 624 Squadron formed at Blida, Algeria, on 22 September 1943 from No. 1575 Special Duties Flight and was assigned to clandestine air operations in the Mediterranean Theatre. Equipped initially with two Venturas and eighteen Halifaxes, its sphere of operations included France, Italy and the Balkans, with occasional trips to Czechoslovakia. Stirlings began to replace the Halifaxes in June 1944, but with southern France and much of Italy now in Allied hands there was less demand for clandestine operations in these areas and the Squadron was disbanded on 5 September. It reformed at Grottaglie on 28 December 1944 and, equipped with Vickers Walrus aircraft, undertook mine-spotting duties around the coasts of Italy and Greece until its disbandment on 30 November 1945.

No. 628 Squadron

No. 628 Squadron formed at Redhills Lake, Madras, from 'B' Flight of No. 357 Squadron on 21 March 1944. Equipped with six Catalina Mk.Ib (and later Mk.IV) aircraft, its task was to infiltrate agents and Force 136 personnel at landing points on the coasts of Burma, Malaya and the Dutch East Indies. Such operations, however, were very sporadic, and the Catalinas were mostly employed on weather reconnaissance and air-sea rescue work until the Squadron's disbandment on 1 October 1944.

No. 419/1419 Flight

Formed at North Weald on 21 August 1940, No. 419 Flight was the first RAF unit formed for clandestine air operations on behalf of SOE and was initially equipped with two Lysanders, two more being held in forward reserve. These were joined in October 1940 by two Whitleys, with a third in reserve. In March 1941 the unit was redesignated No. 1419 Flight, the number 419 having been allocated to an RCAF bomber squadron, and in May the Flight moved to Newmarket, where it provided the nucleus of the newly-formed No. 138 Squadron on 25 August 1941.

No. 1575 Flight

No. 1575 Flight formed at Tempsford on 20 May 1943 with two

Venturas and four Halifaxes to undertake special operations duties in the Mediterranean Theatre. The Flight moved to Blida in North Africa in June 1943 and carried out SD operations over Corsica, Sardinia and Italy. It disbanded on 22 September 1943, its aircraft and personnel forming the nucleus of No. 624 Squadron.

No. 1576 Flight

No. 1576 Flight was formed at Chaklala, India, on 1 June 1943, and was equipped with six Hudsons Mk.III drawn from the Air Landing School, which had been carrying out SD operations on a limited scale. The Flight operated from a forward base at Dum Dum, Calcutta, and carried out SD operations, mainly over Burma, until 1 February 1944, when it was disbanded and reformed immediately as 'A' Flight of No. 357 Squadron.

No. 1586 Flight

Formed in April 1943 from Polish personnel drawn from No. 138 Squadron and No. 301 Squadron, No. 1586 Flight was assigned to special operations in the Mediterranean Theatre, with a particular commitment to Poland. Its aircraft and crews were heavily involved in supplying Home Army forces during the Warsaw Uprising of 1944, and suffered severe losses. On 7 November 1944 the Polish Flight was renumbered 301 Squadron, and under this guise continued SD operations — mainly over Yugoslavia — until 1945, when it returned to the United Kingdom for general transport duties. It was eventually disbanded in December 1946.

Armstrong Whitworth Albemarle
Originally designed as a medium bomber, the Armstrong Whitworth A.W.41 Albemarle prototype flew for the first time on 20 March 1930, but only thirty-two were completed as bombers, and the aircraft never served in its intended role. The original batch was modified for use as transport aircraft, first deliveries being made to No. 295 Squadron at Harwell in January 1943. Subsequent production Albemarles were designated GT (General Transport) or ST (Special Transport) and 566 Mks.I to VI were built. The most widely-used variant was the Mk.VI, of which 250 were constructed. Albemarles saw considerable service in the glider-towing role and large numbers were used in the Allied landings in Sicily, Normandy and at Arnhem. In the special duties role, No. 161 used two Albemarles for a time to carry out various trials, including 'Ascension' radio relay work, but they were classed as unsuitable (mainly through unserviceability) and replaced by Hudsons. However, small numbers of Albemarles were used by RAF transport squadrons to drop supplies to resistance groups in France on behalf of SOE after D-Day, aircraft of Nos. 295, 296, 297 and 570 Squadrons being involved in these operations. The Albemarle had the distinction of being the first British military aircraft with a retractable nosewheel undercarriage.

Engines: Two Bristol Hercules XI radials developing

175

1,590 hp. Span: 77 ft. Length: 59ft 11in. Height: 15ft 7in. Crew: 4. Maximum speed: 265 mph at 10,500 ft. Operational ceiling: 18,000 ft. Range: 1,300 miles. Armament: four .303 machine-guns in dorsal turret.

Armstrong Whitworth Whitley

Designed to Specification B.3/34, the Whitley flew for the first time on 17 March 1936 and the first production aircraft were delivered to No. 10 Squadron, RAF Bomber Command, exactly a year later. Although overshadowed by more modern types such as the Wellington, it performed valuable service during the first two years of the Second World War. Operating mainly with the squadrons of No. 4 Group, it was the first British bomber to attack targets in Italy and also the first to fly over Berlin. The principal wartime variant was the Mk.V, of which 1,466 were built, and 146 Mk.VIIs were also produced for general reconnaissance work with Coastal Command. Although the Whitley was obsolete as a bomber even at the outbreak of war in September 1939, it served as a front-line aircraft until late in 1942, when it was assigned to troop and freight transport duties.

The Whitley's long range — 1,500 miles, compared to the Wellington's 1,300 — made it a logical choice for deep-penetration special duties operations over occupied Europe. Modified to drop agents and supplies by the provision of a simple hole in the fuselage floor, it entered service in this role with No. 419 Flight in October 1940 and subsequently formed the main equipment of Nos. 161 and 138 (Special Duties) Squadrons until replaced by Halifaxes late in 1942.

Engines (Mk.V): Two 1,075 hp Rolls-Royce Merlin X in-lines. Span: 84 ft. Length: 72ft 6in. Height: 15ft. Crew: 5. Maximum speed: 228 mph at 17,750 ft. Operational ceiling: 17,600 ft. Range: 1,500 miles. Armament: five .303 machine-guns and up to 7,000lb of bombs.

Consolidated Catalina

Developed from the civil Model 28 flying boat, the Consolidated PBY-1 Catalina first flew on 21 March 1935 and deliveries began to Navy Squadron VP-11F in October 1936. In 1937-38

176

the PBY-1 was followed by the PBY-2, fifty of which were built, and US Navy orders quickly continued with orders for 66 PBY-3s and 33 PBY-4s, the latter having large observation blisters on either side of the hull. The PBY-5 was an amphibious version and was fitted with a tricycle undercarriage. The last models, the PBY-6 and -6A, had improved armament and increased range.

In 1939 the RAF received a Model 28 for evaluation, and this resulted in a British order for fifty aircraft similar to the US Navy's PBY-5. This order was doubled in 1940, and the RAF eventually received 650 aircraft. Catalinas were used on a limited scale for special operations by Nos. 240, 357 and 628 Squadrons in South-East Asia. In all, 3,290 Catalinas were built, and several hundred more were licence-produced in the Soviet Union under the designation GST.

Engines: Two 1,200 hp Pratt & Whitney Twin Wasp radials. Span: 104ft. Length: 63ft 10in. Height: 20ft 2in. Crew: 8. Maximum speed: 179 mph at 7,000 ft. Operational ceiling: 14,700 ft. Range: 3,100 miles. Armament: five .5in machine-guns. (All details for PBY-5.)

Consolidated B-24 Liberator
Built in considerably greater numbers than its more glamorous counterpart, the B-17 Fortress, the B-24 Liberator — of which 18,188 examples had been produced by the end of May 1945 — first flew on 29 December 1939, by which time orders had already been placed by the US Army Air Corps, France (120) and Great Britain (164). In the summer of 1940 the French order was diverted to Britain, and of the first batch of aircraft to enter British service six went to BOAC for transatlantic ferry work and twenty to RAF Coastal Command for maritime reconnaissance duties as the Liberator I. The RAF also received Liberator IIs, some of which went into action in the bombing role — the first Liberators to do so. The first USAAF Liberator variant to serve as a bomber was the B-24D, of which 2,738 were built; 260 entered RAF service as the Liberator III and IIIA, and a further 122 — with modifications that included chin and ventral radar fairings and a Leigh Light — became Coastal Command's Liberator V.

Liberator IIs were the first RAF variants to be used on special duties operations, with 'X' Flight, No. 148 Squadron and No. 1586 Flight in the Mediterranean, but the Liberator VI was the main variant ultimately used in this role, principally with Nos. 357 and 358 Squadrons in South-East Asia. The RAF received 1,278 Liberator VIs, part of the total of 6,678 B-24Js produced by several American companies. The B-24J was the major production variant, although 3,100 B-24Hs, 1,667 B-24Ls and 2,593 B-24Ms were also built, these variants differing from one another mainly in the type of armament carried.

Although Liberators shared a major part of the USAAF's bombing offensive in Europe with the B-17, their major contribution to the war effort was in the Pacific, where their long range made them particularly suited to far-ranging flights over the ocean. RAF special duties Liberators in South-East Asia were fitted with a slide-type exit for agents and stores, while those in Europe had a circular floor hatch.

> Engines (Liberator VI): Four 1,200 hp Pratt & Whitney Twin Wasp radials. Span: 110ft. Length: 67ft 2in. Height: 18ft. Crew: 12. Maximum speed: 300 mph at 30,000 ft. Operational ceiling: 28,000 ft. Armament: ten .5in machine-guns; 5,000lb of bombs.

Douglas C-47 Dakota

Known as Dakota in RAF service, the twin-engined Douglas C-47 was without doubt the most famous transport aircraft of all time. It flew for the first time on 18 December 1935, and total wartime production — up to August 1945 — was 10,123 aircraft. C-47s served in every theatre of war; about 700 were supplied under Lend-Lease to the Russians, who produced their own version, the Lisunov Li-2.

The RAF received more than 1,200 Dakotas, the first entering service with No. 31 Squadron in Burma in June 1942. No. 267 Squadron, which was to become the RAF's principal Dakota special duties unit in the Middle East, also received its first examples about the same time. Later, No. 267 joined the C-47s of the USAAF's 60th, 62nd and 68th Troop Carrier Groups on special operations from Italian bases.

178

Engines: Two 1,200 hp Pratt & Whitney R-1830
Twin Wasp radials. Span: 95ft. Length: 64ft 5½in.
Height: 16ft 11in. Crew: 4. Passengers: up to 28.
Maximum speed: 230 mph at 8,800 ft. Operational
ceiling: 24,100 ft. Range: 1,350 miles. Armament:
none.

Douglas Havoc
In 1940, the Royal Air Force took over a batch of Douglas DB-7
light bombers which, originally ordered by the Armée de l'Air,
had not been delivered before France's collapse. Named Boston
I and II by the RAF, some of the latter were converted to the
night-fighter and intruder role and renamed Havoc. Variants
included the Havoc I and IV intruders, the Havoc III night-
fighter and a 'Turbinlite' Havoc, fitted with a searchlight in the
nose. These aircraft operated in conjunction with a single-
engined fighter, usually a Hurricane, and illuminated the
target while the fighter attacked it. The Havoc II had its glazed
nose replaced by a solid one mounting twelve .303 machine-
guns.
   A small number of Havoc Is served with No. 161 Squadron
from February 1942 to December 1943 and were employed on
'Ascension' sorties throughout this period. These were designed
to establish and perfect radio relay links with groups of agents
operating in occupied Europe. The Havocs were eventually
replaced in this role by Lockheed Hudsons.

Engines: Two Pratt & Whitney Double Cyclone
radials of 1,600 hp. Span: 61ft 4in. Length: 48ft.
Height: 17ft 7in. Crew: 3. Maximum speed: 320 mph
at 13,000 ft. Operational ceiling: 25,000 ft. Range:
1,050 miles. Armament: two .303 Browning
machine-guns in dorsal position, two on either side of
nose; one Vickers K gun in ventral position.

Handley Page Halifax
Destined, with its famous counterpart, the Lancaster, to play a
major part in the RAF's bombing offensive against Germany,
the Handley Page Halifax was the second four-engined heavy
bomber to enter service with Bomber Command during the

Second World War, the first being the Short Stirling. The prototype Halifax flew on 24 September 1939 and first deliveries were made to No. 35 Squadron in November 1940, the aircraft making its operational debut in a raid on Le Havre on the night of 11/12 March 1941. The Halifax remained in service with Bomber Command throughout the war and served with Coastal and Transport Commands afterwards, the last aircraft being delivered in November 1946. By that time 6,176 had been built.

From the end of 1942 the Halifax replaced the Whitley in the special duties role, and remained the standard long-range type in service with Nos. 138, 148 and 161 Squadrons until it was replaced by Stirlings in 1944. The type was also operated by No. 624 Squadron and the Polish 1586 Flight. The main Halifax variant employed on SD work was the Mk.V Series I (Special), which had appropriate modifications for the dropping of agents and supplies, although No. 138 Squadron used Halifax Is and IIs until it was re-equipped. The most notable differences between the Halifax I, II and V were that they were powered by Rolls-Royce Merlin engines, whereas other marks had Bristol Hercules radials, and the design of the front fuselage and vertical tail surfaces.

> Engines (Mk.I): Four 1,075 hp Rolls-Royce Merlin X 'Vee' Type. Span: 98ft 10in. Length: 70ft 1in. Height: 20ft 9in. Crew: 7. Maximum speed: 265 mph at 17,500 ft. Operational ceiling: 22,800 ft. Range: 1,860 miles. Armament: two .303 Browning machine-guns in nose turret (some SD aircraft had the nose turret deleted) and four in tail turret.

Lockheed Hudson

Originally developed in 1938 to meet a British requirement for a coastal reconnaissance aircraft, the Lockheed Hudson became the first American aircraft to see action in the Second World War. An RAF order was placed for 200, and the first of these flew in December 1938, first deliveries being made to No. 224 Squadron in May 1939. The RAF had 78 Hudsons on the outbreak of war, and subsequent deliveries increased the eventual total (Hudsons Mk.I-VI) to just under 2,000 aircraft. These achieved some notable 'firsts' in RAF service, including the destruction of the first enemy aircraft to fall to the RAF in the Second World War, on 8 October 1939, the locating of the infamous German prison ship 'Altmark', and the first sinking of a U-Boat with rocket projectiles.

The first Hudson to be assigned to special operations was N7263, formerly of the King's Flight, which remained on the strength of No. 161 Squadron from 1942 until 1944. Hudsons were used extensively by this Squadron for pickup operations and — on a more limited scale — for supply dropping. Hudsons, too, carried out the first clandestine air operations in South-East Asia, operating with No. 1576 Flight at Chaklala, India, and with No. 357 Squadron. In US service, the Hudson was designated A-28 and A-29, and some A-28s were transferred to the US Navy under the designation PBO-1. One of the latter machines, flying with Squadron VP-82, became the first US aircraft to destroy a German submarine.

Engines (Hudson Mk.III): Two 1,200 hp Wright Cyclone radials. Span: 65ft 6in. Length: 44ft 4in. Height: 11ft 10½in. Crew: 5 (2 or 3 on SD operations). Maximum speed: 255 mph at 5,000 feet. Operational ceiling: 24,500 ft. Range: 2,160 miles. Armament: up to seven .303in machine-guns and up to 750lb of bombs.

Lockheed Ventura
Designed to meet a British requirement for a successor to the Hudson, the Lockheed Ventura was evolved from the civilian Lockheed Model 18 airliner and first flew on 31 July 1941. Initial RAF orders were for 675 aircraft, and the first Ventura Mk.Is entered service with No. 21 Squadron, Bomber Command, in October 1942. Other light bomber squadrons in No. 2 Group to use the Ventura were Nos. 464 (RAAF) and 487 (RNZAF), and many daylight attacks were made on pinpoint targets in France and the Low Countries before the type was replaced by Mosquitos in the autumn of 1943.

In May 1943, two Venturas were allocated to No. 1575 (Special Duties) Flight, and these carried out SD operations over Corsica, Italy and Sardinia from bases in North Africa. They also served for a period with No. 624 Squadron after the latter's formation in September 1943.

> Engines: Two 2,000 hp Pratt & Whitney Double
> Wasp radials. Span: 65ft 6in. Length: 51ft 9in.
> Height: 13ft 2in. Crew: 4. Maximum speed: 315 mph
> at 15,200 ft. Operational ceiling: 27,500 ft. Range:
> 1,100 miles. Armament: two .303 machine-guns in
> nose, four .303 machine-guns in dorsal and ventral
> positions (two each); up to 2,500lb of bombs or
> supplies.

Short Stirling

Although the Stirling was the first four-engined Allied bomber
to serve in the Second World War, its effectiveness was limited
by its low aspect ratio wings, which restricted its operational
ceiling and also its bomb load. The wing design was an unhappy
feature of Specification B.12/36, which required the new
bomber to be able to fit into existing hangars.

The first Stirling flew on 14 May 1939 but crashed on landing,
and it was August 1940 before the first deliveries were made
to No. 7 Squadron, RAF Bomber Command. Stirlings subsequently equipped thirteen heavy bomber squadrons, and
during 1941 the type carried out a series of daylight raids on
targets in occupied Europe. With an increase in enemy fighter
opposition, daylight raids were abandoned in 1942 and the
effort of the Stirling squadrons was turned over to night
operations.

A total of 2,375 Stirlings was produced during the war, the
major production version being the Mk.III, of which 875 were
built. In 1943, two Mk.IIIs were converted as prototypes of the
Mk.IV, and this version was to see widespread service in the
transport and glider-tug roles. In the summer of 1944, Stirling
IVs (and some Mk.IIIs) began to replace the Halifaxes of Nos.
138, 148, 161 and 624 Squadrons in the special duties role, for
which they were equipped with an exit hatch aft of the bomb
bay. Special duties Stirlings had all gun positions removed
except the rear gun turret.

The final Stirling variant was the Mk.V, which was also a
transport. It featured a lengthened 'solid' nose, and 160 were
built, some serving for two or three years after the war's end.

Engines: Four 1,650 hp Bristol Hercules XVI radials. Span: 99ft 1in. Length: 87ft 3in. Height: 22ft 9in. Crew: 5, 7 or 8, depending on role. Maximum speed: 270 mph at 14,500 ft. Operational ceiling: 17,000 ft. Range: 2,000 miles. Armament (SD Mk.IV): four .303 Browning machine-guns in tail turret.

Westland Lysander
The most famous of all aircraft employed in special duties work, the Lysander began life as a two-seat Army co-operation aircraft, the prototype flying for the first time on 15 June 1936. An initial order was placed for 144 machines, and deliveries began in June 1938 to No. 16 Squadron. Lysanders were widely used in France and the Middle East during the early war years and the Army co-operation squadrons suffered considerable casualties during the German *Blitzkrieg* of May 1940. The original order for Mk.Is was later increased to 169, and these were followed by 442 Mk.IIs, 267 Mk.IIIs and 447 Mk.IIIAs. Production ceased in January 1942, when the Curtiss P-40 Tomahawk began to replace the Lysander in the Army co-operation squadrons, but the Lysander went on to serve in various other roles, including that of target tug and air-sea-rescue spotter.

The factors that made the Lysander eminently suited to special duties pickup operations were as follows:

a. Considerable weight-lifting capacity.
b. Low landing speed in a natural three-point attitude.
c. Automatic flap action, meeting all the conditions of flight — for example, a sudden loss of lift in conditions of turbulence, or in a sudden violent turn.
d. A high rate of turn, of great value in confined spaces.
e. The ability to cruise at low speed in conditions of poor visibility.
f. A fixed undercarriage, very strong and specifically designed to withstand the shock of continual heavy landings on rough ground in forward areas.
g. High engine power, facilitating quick take-off from water-logged strips, with an immediate high rate of climb.
h. Excellent visibility for the pilot when map reading.

i.   Duration of flight; in the SD role, the 98-gallon fuel tank situated behind the pilot's cockpit was supplemented by a 150-gallon torpedo-shaped auxiliary tank, slung under the fuselage.

Other modifications to SD Lysanders included the removal of the short stub wings (used for the mounting of bombs or guns in the Army co-operation role) from the aircraft's undercarriage spats, and the provision of a fixed metal ladder to the port side of the fuselage to facilitate access to the rear cockpit. SD Lysanders in Europe were at first camouflaged matt black, but this was later changed back to standard dark green and pale grey as the black paintwork made a dangerous silhouette against low cloud. Lysanders used for special duties work in South-East Asia — which usually operated in daylight — carried green/brown camouflage throughout.

> Engine (Mk.III): One 870 hp Bristol Mercury 30 radial. Span: 50ft. Length: 30ft 6in. Height: 14ft 6in. Crew: 1 or 2, depending on role. Passengers: up to 4. Maximum speed: 212 mph at 5,000 ft. Operational ceiling: 21,500 ft. Range: 800 miles with auxiliary tank. Armament: none (Army co-operation aircraft carried four .303 machine-guns and up to six small bombs).

Note: Various other aircraft types were evaluated for special operations during the Second World War. These included the Martin Maryland, Vickers Wellington and Avro Anson, the latter being used to carry out one pickup operation. In South-East Asia, some pickup operations were carried out by Stinson L-5 aircraft.

(FTR = Failed to return)
No. 161 Squadron — Representative Aircraft, 1942

*Armstrong Whitworth
  Albemarle I*
P1378
P1390

*Armstrong Whitworth
  Whitley V*
Z6653 (FTR, 2/3.10.42)
Z6747
Z6828
Z6940 (FTR, 20.9.42)
Z9224
Z9438
BD202
BD223
BD228 (FTR, September
  1942)
BD267
BD363

Douglas Havoc I
AW399

Handley Page Halifax V
W1046
DG244
DG245
DG285
DG286

Vickers Wellington I
P2521

Westland Lysander III
T1770
V9367
V9428
V9595
V9597 (Burnt, 1.9.42)

BJ477

No. 148 Squadron: Allocation of Aircraft, January 1943

Liberator II

AL506	AL510
AL509	AL530

No. 148 Squadron: Aircraft on Charge, January 1944

Handley Page Halifax II/V

BB302 'H'	HR660 'A'
BB335 'J'	JN888
BB381 'O'	JN896 'L'
BB388 'Q'	JN898
BB421 'R'	JN925
BB422 'S'	JN956 'E'
BB431	JN959 'N'
BB438	
BB445	*Liberator II*
BB481	AL510 'W'

No. 138 Squadron: Stirling Allocations, 1944-45

Stirling Mk.IV

LJ990	LK143	LK200	LK272
LJ993	LK145	LK204	LK274
LJ999	LK149	LK206	LK278
LK119	LK151	LK207	LK283
LK125	LK192	LK208	LK285
LK131	LK194	LK209	LK309
	LK198	LK210	LK329

APPENDIX 4: No. 138 SQUADRON CASUALTIES, 1942-45

(FTR = Failed to return)

Aircraft	Date	Captain	Remarks
Whitley V	29 January 1942	Not known	FTR France
Halifax I	10 March 1942	Sqn Ldr B. Romanoff	FTR France
Halifax I	28 March 1942	Plt Off S. Widdup	FTR France
Whitley V	20 April 1942	Sgt Wilde	FTR France
Whitley V	21 April 1942	Sgt Shaddick	
Halifax I	21 April 1942	Wng Cdr W.R. Farley	
Halifax I	1 October 1942	Not known	W7776. Crash-landed near Whitby on return from ops
Halifax I	30 October 1942	Not known	W7773. FTR
Halifax I	30 October 1942	Not known	W7774. Ditched off Sheringham, Norfolk with battle damage
Halifax II	7 December 1942	Flg Off Idzikowski	FTR Czechoslovakia
Halifax I	10 December 1942	Not known	L9618. Missing in flight to Malta
Halifax I	10 December 1942	Not known	W1002. Crashed in Western Desert
Halifax II	15 December 1942	Flg Off M. Anderle	FTR
Halifax II	17 December 1942	Not known	DT542. Crashed on landing at Luqa, Malta
Halifax I	23 December 1942	Plt Off N. Tinley	W7775. FTR
Halifax II	20 February 1943	Plt Off Kingsford Smith	FTR France
Halifax II	15 March 1943	Sqn Ldr Gibson	FTR Czechoslovakia
Halifax II	15 March 1943	Flt Sgt Smith	DT620. FTR Denmark en route to Poland

187

Aircraft	Date	Captain	Remarks
Halifax II	25 March 1943	Not known	FTR (France?)
Halifax II	13 April 1943	Flg Off Izycki	BB340. FTR
Halifax II	14 April 1943	Not known	BB363. FTR
Halifax II	17 April 1943	Flg Off Lawrenczuk	DT725. FTR
Halifax II	14 May 1943	Not known	BB313. FTR
Halifax II	18 May 1943	Not known	JB802. Crashed after hitting house at Maison Blanche
Halifax II	22 May 1943	Flt Sgt P.B. Norris	BB328. FTR
Halifax II	22 June 1943	Not known	DT727. Hit hangar at Tempsford
Halifax II	24 June 1943	Flt Sgt T. Zabicki	BB379. FTR
Halifax II	12 July 1943	Flt Lt J. Morawski	JD155. FTR
Halifax II	13 August 1943	W/O R.A. Scott	BB334. FTR
Halifax II	15 August 1943	Sqn Ldr F.C. Griffiths	JD180. FTR Annecy
Halifax II	17 August 1943	Flg Off J.A. Krzehlik	JD312. FTR Poland
Halifax II	18 August 1943	Flt Sgt N.W. Hayter	JD179. FTR France
Halifax II	18 August 1943	Not known	DG253. Crashed on landing at Tempsford
Halifax II	20 August 1943	Flt Lt R.P. Wilkin	FTR
Halifax II	20 August 1943	Flt Sgt N.L. Sherwood	FTR
Halifax II	15 September 1943	Flg Off A.J. Milne	HR666. FTR Poland
Halifax II	15 September 1943	Flt Lt F. Jakusz-Gostomski	JD269. FTR Poland
Halifax II	15 September 1943	Flg Off E.C. Hart	JN910. FTR Holland
Halifax II	15 September 1943	Sgt W.H. James	JD154. FTR Holland
Halifax II	17 September 1943	Flt Sgt L.A. Trotter	JD156. FTR Holland
Halifax II	17 September 1943	Flt Sgt T. Miecznik	BB309. FTR Denmark
Halifax II	20 September 1943	Not known	DG252. FTR Denmark
Halifax II	20 September 1943	Not known	BB317. FTR
Halifax II	10 October 1943	W/O B. Hulas	FTR
Halifax II	19 October 1943	Sqn Ldr C. Passy	LW281. FTR
Halifax II	4 November 1943	Captain J. Estes, USAAF	FTR
Halifax II	7 November 1943	Flt Sgt K.R. Kopas	JN921. FTR
Halifax II	11 December 1943	Flt Lt A.C. Bartter	BB378. Crash-landed in Denmark after attack by BF110
Halifax II	17 December 1943	Flt Sgt J.J. Watson	LL115. Crashed into wood near Woodbridge on return from ops
Halifax II	17 December 1943	Not known	LL119. Crew bailed out and aircraft crashed in sea off Felixstowe
Halifax II	17 December 1943	Not known	LL120. Crew bailed out and aircraft crashed in sea off Skegness

Aircraft	Date	Captain	Remarks
Halifax II	17 December 1943	Not known	LW280. Aircraft crashed in sea off Essex coast in bad weather
Halifax II	19 December 1943	Sgt H.D. Williams	BB364. Aircraft hit chimney and crashed near Henlow
Halifax II	8 January 1944	W/O H.M. Kennedy	LK743. Crashed at Tetworth Hill, Bedford
Halifax II	8 February 1944	Flt Lt T.C. Cooke	LL114. FTR France
Halifax II	8 February 1944	Flg Off C.D. Carroll	FTR
Halifax II	4 March 1944	Not known	LL279. FTR
Halifax II	31 March 1944	Not known	LL287. FTR
Halifax II	1 April 1944	Flg Off F.B. Clark	LL252. FTR
Halifax II	3 April 1944	Flg Off W.C. Kingsley	FTR
Halifax II	28 April 1944	Not known	LL356. FTR
Halifax II	8 May 1944	Sqn Ldr W.M. Russell	LL192. Crashed in Kattegat
Halifax II	8 May 1944	Flg Off H.H. McMullen	LL280. FTR
Halifax II	9 May 1944	Flg Off H.S. Coldridge	FTR
Halifax II	17 May 1944	Not known	LK736. Crash-landed following engine fire at Great Barford, Bedford
Halifax II	1 June 1944	Flg Off J.P. Gallagher	LL276. FTR
Halifax II	2 June 1944	W/O H.F.G. Murray	LL284. Crashed on take-off for ops, Tempsford
Halifax II	2 June 1944	Plt Off D.A. Hayman	LL289. FTR
Halifax II	3 June 1944	Plt Off T.M. Thomas	LL307. FTR
Halifax II	8 June 1944	Flg Off F.H. Lyne	LL306. FTR
Halifax II	8 June 1944	Plt Off H.C. Jones	LL466. FTR
Halifax II	8 June 1944	Flt Sgt A.D. McKay	LL390. Hit pillbox on take-off from Tempsford
Halifax II	12 July 1944	Not known	LL251. FTR
Halifax II	17 July 1944	Not known	DT543. Crashed on night flying detail
Halifax II	18 July 1944	Flg Off J.A. Kidd	LL364. FTR
Halifax II	18 July 1944	Flg Off N.L. St.G. Pleasance	LL387. FTR
Stirling IV	9 August 1944	Flt Sgt A.W. Paterson	
Halifax II	30 August 1944	Not known	JD171. FTR
Stirling IV	1 September 1944	Flg Off A.J. Wallace	LK131. FTR Holland
Stirling IV	1 September 1944	Plt Off R.B. Hardie	
Stirling IV	9 September 1944	Flt Lt G.M. Rothwell	LK200. FTR France
Stirling IV	29 September 1944	Not known	Damaged by enemy aircraft and scrapped
Stirling IV	9 November 1944	Flt Lt F.J. Ford	LJ993. FTR Norway

189

Aircraft	Date	Captain	Remarks
Stirling IV	9 November 1944	W/O L.A. Quellette	LK198. FTR Norway
Stirling IV	27 November 1944	Flt Lt R.R. Witham	
Stirling IV	3 December 1944	Not known	LK143
Stirling IV	31 December 1944	Flg Off R. McGregor	LK283. FTR Norway
Stirling IV	10 February 1945	Not known	LK279. FTR Denmark
Stirling IV	24 February 1945	Not known	LK149. FTR Norway
Stirling IV	27 February 1945	Not known	LK272. FTR Norway
Stirling IV	5 March 1945	Not known	LJ999. FTR Denmark
Stirling IV	23 March 1945	Not known	LK209. FTR Holland
Stirling IV	31 March 1945	Not known	LK144. FTR Norway

APPENDIX 5: CLANDESTINE AIR OPERATIONS, SOUTH-EAST ASIA: SELECTED DATA

1. No. 357 Squadron — Aircraft on Charge, 1 February 1945

Liberator VI	Dakota IV	Harvard	Auster
KM160 'W'	KJ914 'O'	FS794	MJ381
KM166 'S'	KJ920 'G'		
KM273 'R'	KJ922 'J'		
KM313 'V'	KJ925 'L'		
KM391 'Y'	KJ889 'D'		
KM216 'Z'	KJ919 'F'		
KM257 'Q'	KJ921 'H'		
KM326 'X'	KJ924 'K'		
KM323 'U'	KJ926 'M'		
KM395 'P'	KJ490 'N'		
KM325	KJ913		

Note: Aircraft listed in order as taken on charge.

2. No. 358 Squadron — Aircraft on Charge, 1 February 1945

Liberator VI

KH312 'X'	KH282 'G'
KG925 'U'	KH277 'Z'
KG977 'L'	KH167 'A'
KH278 'W'	KH253 'O'

KH367 'Q'	KH350 'T'
KH271 'C'	KH257 'H'
KH353 'D'	KH365 'N'
KH215 'K'	

3. No. 357 Squadron Lysander Flight — Allocation of Aircraft

V9494
V9818
V9295 (Destroyed by storm, Meiktila, 6 May 1945)
V9649 (Destroyed by storm, Meiktila, 6 May 1945)
V9495 (Written off after landing accident)
T1699 (Destroyed by storm, Meiktila, 6 May 1945)
V9808 (Lost on operations, 16 May 1945)
V9889 (Crashed on Amherst Beach, 3 September 1945)
V9815 (Stricken off after damage on operational sortie, 4 August 1945)
V9665 (Crashed on take-off at Mingaladon, 26 October 1945)
V9867
V9289
V9885 (Crashed at Lipyekhi, 24 August 1945)
T1532
V9303 (Damaged on operations, 24 September 1945)

4. Personnel and Stores Carried by Lysander Flight, May-November 1945

Month	Personnel in	Personnel out	Stores landed or dropped (lbs)
May	8	15	2,975
June	9	46	14,995
July	26	56	27,240
August	37	36	23,490
September	77	110	17,240
	(65 Force 136)	(61 Force 136, 49 PoW)	
October	42	54	16,605
November (1-6)	15	13	2,035

Note: The above totals do not include personnel inter-communicating between landing strips.

5. Description of Typical Landing Strip

Usually a stretch of cleared and levelled paddy 450 by 50 yards, with obstacles on approaches cleared. Strips were prepared with the help of local villagers. Elephants were sometimes used.

Identification: white code letters (parachute cloth or bleached bamboo strips), e.g. 'W.T.'

Permission to land: denoted by a white letter 'X'.

Danger signal ('Do not land'): white letter 'M', or alternatively strip markings placed in disorder.

Wind direction indication: white 'T' showing recommended direction of approach. Smoke flares were lit as aircraft approached the target. An extra aid was a small windsock on a pole.

After landing: armed guards were placed on the aircraft. If the Japanese were within a few miles, armed guards and patrols were stationed at all approaches to the strip.

Stores: after unloading, these were placed in a bamboo 'basha' beside the strip to await collection and distribution.

After V.J. Day the following improvements were added: the name of the strip in bold white letters on the ground, e.g. MEWAING AIRPORT, and 'tea and cakes' in a special 'basha' denoted on a signboard as '357 Squadron Canteen'.

6. Aircrew of 'C' Flight, 357 Squadron — Operational Record in Burma

Rank/Name	Operational Hours	Pickups	Free Drops	Remarks
Sqn Ldr. G.A. Turner	197.50	69	16	Returned to UK, January 1946
Flt Lt P. Arkell	96.25	21	14	Injured in crash and returned to UK August 1945
Flg Off P.L. Darlington	86.30 (as pilot) 76.35 (as despatcher)	8	29	
Flg Off H.V.D. Hallett	86.55 (as despatcher)	?	?	Returned to UK, November 1945
Flt Sgt R. Castledine	223.05 (as pilot) 30.15 (as despatcher)	72	19	
Flt Sgt S.H.A. Stubbings	207.20 (as pilot) 14.20 (as despatcher)	52	30	

Rank/Name	Operational Hours	Pickups	Free Drops	Remarks
Flt Sgt T.N. Hall	107.25 (as pilot) 10.30 (as despatcher)	24	16	
Flt Sgt K.B.D. Stamp	78.20 (as pilot) 63.15 (as despatcher)	2	30	
Flt Sgt M.W. Haggar	99.50 (as despatcher)	—	37	
Sgt B. Scott	43.50 (as despatcher)	—	18	
Sgt W.N. Bowley	43.25 (as despatcher)	—	19	
Sgt E. Cross	30.00 (as despatcher)	—	16	

Note: The last four NCOs, although General Duties Pilots, were not trained as Lysander pilots.

SELECT BIBLIOGRAPHY

Bowen, John. *Undercover in the Jungle.* William Kimber, 1978
Buckmaster, Maurice. *They Fought Alone: the Story of British Agents in France.* Odhams Press, 1958
Cookridge, E.H. *Inside SOE: the Story of Special Operations in Western Europe, 1940-45.* Arthur Barker, 1966
Davidson, Basil. *Special Operations Europe: Scenes from the Anti-Nazi War.* Gollancz, 1980
Foot, M.R.D. *SOE in France: an Account of the Work of the British Special Operations Executive in France, 1940-44.* HMSO, 1966
Fuller, Jean Overton. *The German Penetration of SOE: France 1941-44.* William Kimber, 1975
Garlinski, Josef. *Hitler's Last Weapons: the Underground War against V-1 and V-2.* Julian Friedmann, 1978
Griffiths, Frank. *Winged Hours.* William Kimber, 1981
Hamilton-Hill, Donald. *SOE Assignment.* William Kimber, 1973
Haukelid, Knut. *Skis Against the Atom.* William Kimber, 1954
Howarth, Patrick. *Undercover: the Men and Women of the Special Operations Executive.* Routledge and Kegan Paul, 1980
Irving, David. *The Virus House.* William Kimber, 1967
Jackson, Robert. *Heroines of World War Two.* Arthur Barker, 1974
Johns, Philip. *Within Two Cloaks: Missions with SIS and SOE.* William Kimber, 1979
Kemp, Peter. *No Colours or Crest.* Cassell, 1958
Le Chene, Evelyn. *Watch for me by Moonlight: a British Agent with the French Resistance.* Eyre Methuen, 1973

McCall, Gibb. *Flight Most Secret: Air Missions for SOE and SIS.* William Kimber, 1981

MacCluskey, Brigadier General Monro. *Secret Air Missions.* Richards Rosen Press, 1966

Minney, R.J. *Carve Her Name With Pride.* George Newnes, 1956

Nesbitt-Dufort, John. *Black Lysander.* Jarrolds, 1973

Piquet-Wicks, Eric. *Four in the Shadows: a True Story of Espionage in Occupied France.* Jarrolds, 1957

Stafford, David. *Britain and European Resistance 1940-45: a Survey of the Special Operations Executive.* Macmillan, 1980

Sweet-Escott, Bickham. *Baker Street Irregular: Five Years in the Special Operations Executive.* Methuen, 1965

Tickell, Jerrard. *Moon Squadron.* Allan Wingate, 1956

Trenowden, Ian. *Operations Most Secret: SOE — the Malayan Theatre.* William Kimber, 1978

Verity, Hugh. *We Landed by Moonlight.* Ian Allan, 1978

Walters, Anne-Marie. *Moondrop to Gascony.* Macmillan, 1946

Index

197